GRADES 2-6

The Seven C's of Thinking Clearly

Character Based Learning Activities
for Developing Emotional, Social, and Thinking Skills

BY GEORGE L. ROGERS

ILLUSTRATED BY GERALD ROGERS

ChoiceSkills • P.O. Box 54 • Midvale, Utah

www.choiceskills.com

Publisher's Cataloging-in-Publication
(Provided by Quality Books, Inc.)

Rogers, George L., 1938-
  The seven C's of thinking clearly, grades 2-6 : character based learning activities for developing emotional, social, and thinking skills / by George L. Rogers ; illustrated by Gerald Rogers. -- 1st ed.
    p. cm.
    Includes index.
    LCCN 2001094621
    ISBN 0-938399-12-8

  1. Thought and thinking--Study and teaching Elementary)--United States. 2. Social skills--Study and teaching (Elementary)--United States. 3. Education, Elementary--Activity programs--United States. I. Rogers Gerald, 1974- II. Title.

LB1590.3.R64 2002   372.13
                               QBI98-500019

NOTE: Every effort has been made to identify the author and or copyright holder for every story and activity in this book. In those instances where it has not been possible to do so, I have noted the article as "Author Unknown." Should the reader happen to know the source of any of these stories, I will be happy to correct future editions.

Although only some selections are so noted, I am the author, though not necessarily the originator, of all other stories, biographical sketches, and activities in this book.

The Seven C's of Thinking Clearly

for Grades 2-6

Character Based Learning Activities
for Developing Emotional, Social, and Thinking Skills

Such as are thy habitual thoughts,
such also will be the character of thy mind;
for the soul is dyed by the thoughts.
Marcus Aurelius

TABLE OF CONTENTS

INTRODUCTION

When teaching workshops for parents and teachers, I often begin with an exercise titled, "Qualities I would Most Like to See My Students (or Children) Possess."

The results are always the same. In ranking ten qualities from most to least important, excelling in music, sports, or some other field of interest is among the least important. So also is high academic achievement.

The qualities parents and teachers most want children to possess are things like dependability, responsibility, and honesty. They want their children to be caring, decent people who are emotionally and socially competent. True they would like to see them do well in their chosen fields of interest, but most of all, they want their children to be happy, well-adjusted human beings.

It seems, most parents and teachers would agree with the advice Benjamin Franklin gave a young friend who had become interested in the study of insects. After commending her for her interest, he wrote,

"There is, however, a prudent moderation to be used in studies of this kind. The knowledge of nature may be ornamental, and it may be useful; but if, to attain an eminence in that, we neglect the knowledge and practice of essential duties, we deserve reprehension. For there is no rank in natural knowledge of equal dignity and importance with that of being a good parent, a good child, a good husband or wife, a good neighbor or friend, a good subject or citizen. . . ."

Benjamin Franklin's The Art of Virtue, p. 40

In 1728, Franklin wrote an article for the *Weekly Mercury* in which he commented on the role of educational institutions in fostering these qualities.

"It is said that the Persians, in their constitution, had public schools in which virtue was taught as a liberal art or science; and it is certainly of more consequence to a man that he has learnt to govern his passions in spite of temptation, to be just in his dealings, to be temperate in his pleasures, to support himself with fortitude under his misfortunes, to behave with prudence in all his affairs and every circumstance of life; I say, it is of much more real advantage to him to be thus qualified, than to be master of all the arts and sciences in the world besides."

p. 21

But, how do you teach children to govern their passions and to be good neighbors and citizens? How do you teach them to be just in their dealings, temperate in their pleasures, and to behave with prudence? How do you teach them these qualities without constantly lecturing, nagging, scolding and punishing them?

The first answer, of course, is in modeling these qualities ourselves so they can see what they look like. The next answer is to provide them with character based learning experiences wherein they come to understand the immense value of these qualities and desire to possess them.

Character based learning is learning in which students are:

1) Acquiring useful knowledge
2) Developing their thinking skills, and
3) Strengthening their character

all at the same time, or as part of the same learning experience.

The acquisition of knowledge, is the first business of youth. And, though most young people don't realize it, the knowledge they acquire in this season of their lives is the foundation on which they must build for the future. This is not only important for them personally, it is also critical to the future of the societies in which they live. Gaining a solid understanding of the arts and sciences is not merely an amusing pastime, it is serious business and begins at an early age. Individuals and nations who are unsuccessful in this endeavor are severely disadvantaged.

The strengthening of one's character is no less an essential ingredient in one's education. Mutual respect for one another is a primal ingredient for a happy and productive life and an essential glue in holding communities and nations together. But mutual respect can only exist where there is mutual trust and where individuals take personal responsibility for their choices and actions.

The development of thinking skills is fundamental to both the acquisition of knowledge and the strengthening of one's character. Neither can fully occur without well developed thinking skills.

Here we are not talking about intellectual capacity. It is possible to be very bright without being very wise. We're talking about the kind of thinking skills Benjamin Franklin was referring to when he wrote: ". . .as the happiness or real good of men consists in right action, and right action cannot be produced without right opinion, it behooves us, above all things in this world, to take care that our own opinions of things be according to the nature of things. The foundation of all virtue and happiness is thinking rightly." *Benjamin Franklin's the Art of Virtue, page 29.*

These kind of thinking skills, the kind that enable us to think rightly, involve not only the head but also the heart.

In fact, the seven C skills in *The Seven C's of Thinking Clearly* are specific skills Franklin consciously developed in his own life, skills that encompass both head and heart. Notwithstanding Franklin was one of the brightest men to have ever lived, he didn't trust human reason, ". . .since it enables one to find or make a reason for everything

one has a mind to do."

Character based learning can be experienced while learning how to read or write, how to add or subtract, how to play a game, or how to put away one's clothes. Character based learning can be experienced while learning about health, science, history, music, woodworking or any of the myriad things we are constantly teaching children to do.

For example, virtually every game has rules. Why? Because rules make games fun. In hide 'n go seek, if the person who is "it" doesn't count to fifty, the other players feel cheated and no longer want to play. Rules are necessary to provide structure to the game and to assure that everyone has a fair chance to win. When the element of fair chance is taken away, the game ceases to be fun.

So, when playing games with children, what if we go beyond simply explaining what the rules are and take a little time, it doesn't take much, to explore with children why the rules exist in the first place. A couple of simple questions will do it: "Why do you suppose the game needs this rule?" "What do you think would happen if the game didn't have this rule?" "Why do we need to agree upon the rules we are going to play by?" etc. A discussion of this kind can accomplish several things.

1) We help them enjoy the game more.
2) We help them better understand the concept of fairness.
3) We help them better understand why we have rules at home, school and elsewhere.
4) And we have provided them with an exercise in critical thinking and hopefully, stimulated their curiosity.

While each section in *The Seven C's of Thinking Clearly* has a particular focus, every lesson is designed to provide you with a mini-tutorial in creating character based learning experiences for your children and students.

First of all, each lesson has a learning component such as reading, writing, social studies, science, etc. which you will find to be supportive of, if not directly related to, core curriculum requirements in your state. Next, every lesson has a character strengthening component and provides an opportunity to explore, discuss, or develop specific character traits. Finally, each lesson has a thinking skills component.

Since, thinking skills are at the root of both the acquisition of knowledge and character development, the *Seven C's of Thinking Clearly* is organized as follows.

Section One is primarily focused on recognizing faulty thinking habits or practices that inhibit personal progress.

For young people to fully appreciate the need to develop the seven C skills, it is necessary for them to be able to recognize the problems created by faulty thinking. They need to understand both its causes and its various manifestations. To accomplish this in a manner that is interesting and fun, six types of faulty thinking are presented in this book as The Stink'n Think'n Gang, a band of thieves out to rob us of common sense and good judgment.

Section two is devoted to learning about the seven C skills—Criticism, Creativity, Communication, Concentration, Curiosity, Correction, and Control. Lessons in this section are focused on learning what these skills are and understanding the importance of consciously developing them in one's own life.

Hindsight, Insight, and Foresight questions designed provide practical exercises in critical thinking follow nearly every lesson.

Hindsight Questions are used to help young people learn from experience—their own experience and the experiences of others. All too many youth go through life as if no one has ever lived before, repeating mistakes of the past, and suffering what could have been avoided had they paid more attention to what others have experienced.

Insight Questions are used to help young people understand why things are the way they are; to help them probe more deeply into the nature of things. The purpose of the insight questions is to help them gain a larger perspective with respect to choices they make.

Foresight Questions are used to help young people learn how to anticipate the probable or likely consequences of their choices.

If we can help young people develop the discipline of looking back at the past to see what has happened, to look at the nature of what it is they are contemplating doing, and to anticipate the possible outcomes, they will be in a much stronger position to make responsible choices.

Sections Three through Six focus on the character traits of personal responsibility, self-respect, respect for others, and trustworthiness. The specifics of these traits are covered in more detail on the following page.

While lessons from any section may be presented in any order, you will note that each section builds on the other. Section One identifies a serious problem that afflicts most of us, frankly, and accounts for a large portion of the unhappiness we experience. The remaining sections build a foundation for solving that problem.

This scaffolding approach to the sections is simply for purposes of focus. Most lessons are in fact multidimensional and can be presented from more than one point of view, ie. it can be used to discuss more than one thinking skill and it can be used to discuss more than one character trait. In fact, one of the best uses of these lessons is to consider them from more than one point of view on more than one occasion.

Whether you are teaching these lessons at school, in the home, a youth organization, or somewhere else—they have been designed to be easily prepared and interestingly presented. Most lessons can be prepared in a matter of minutes and be presented in a variety of ways. For example, many lessons may be presented in a 20-minute block, two 10-minute blocks, or four 5-minute blocks. Where advance preparation is required, the requirements are noted by the words ADVANCE PREPARATION with a description of the preparation required.

An Index to the rich literature base contained in this book may be found on pages 171 and 173 under the headings "Great Lessons From Great Lives" and "Great Lessons From Great Literature." You will find these stories, not only entertaining, but also inspiring reading. They will provide you many ideas on how you might want to approach the lessons contained herein.

Character Trait Reference Guide

The Seven C's of Thinking Clearly books each contain over 120 character based learning activities for helping children develop their emotional, social, and thinking skills. Each activity provides a context and opportunity for discussing one or more character traits with your students. The character traits each story or activity best illustrates are noted in the discussion opportunity box associated with the activity. Most stories and many activities provide opportunities for discussion of multiple character traits. For example, the notation "Character Traits: PR ownership; SR self-reliance; T dependability" indicates that this particular activity or story provides discussion opportunities for 1) taking ownership of your choices, 2) exercising initiative, and 3) being dependable. In some cases you may choose to discuss all of the relevant character traits in one discussion. In other situations, you may choose to only consider one character trait at a time. It is often advantageous to revisit a story or activity more than once to discuss it from a different angle or point of view. Once young people begin to realize that many stories have multiple levels of meaning or lessons to be learned, their reading experiences will become richer and more meaningful.

If you are looking for an activity or story to teach a particular character trait, refer to the Character Trait Cross Reference Index on page 164.

Character Traits Referenced in The Seven C's of Thinking Clearly

Personal Responsibility - Taking Ownership
- The ability to act
- The right to act
- The duty to act
- Accepting accountability

Self-Respect
- Self-Understanding
- Self-Discipline
- Self-Reliance
    - Initiative
    - Industriousness
    - Persistence
    - Patience
    - Resourcefulness

Respect for Others
- Caring
- Fairness
- Citizenship
    - Honoring laws
    - Honoring legitimate authority
    - Honoring the rights of others
    - Honoring the property of others
    - Honoring the environment

Trustworthiness
- Honesty
- Dependability

1

CHOOSING
TO AVOID
FAULTY THINKING

Section One

ॐ

LEARNING OBJECTIVES FOR SECTION ONE

The ability to recognize six types of faulty thinking

An appreciation of the difficulties caused by faulty thinking

It leads people to want things that aren't good for them

It leads people to not want things that are good for them

It leads people to overvalue or undervalue the importance of things

It leads people to be dishonest with each other

It leads people to form opinions contrary to the nature of things

A desire to develop safeguards against faulty thinking in all its forms

SECTION OVERVIEW

Benjamin Franklin once wrote, ". . . .as the happiness or real good of men consists in right action and right action cannot be produced without right opinion, it behooves us, above all things in this world to take care that our own opinions of things be according to the nature of things. The foundation of all virtue and happiness is thinking rightly." (*Benjamin Franklin's The Art of Virtue*, pp. 29, 30)

Unfortunately, there are several common, even prevalent, thinking habits which are faulty at the core and inhibit our ability to think clearly. They are faulty because they alter, distort, or ignore information necessary to forming a correct understanding of the nature of things. People who indulge in them are vulnerable to making choices that complicate and sometimes ruin their lives. In this book we focus on six habits of stink'n think'n, presented as members of the Stink'n Think'n Gang. They are Iwannit Now, Biggs Bigger, Eency Wency Tiny Too, Li Fib, Nameit Blameit, and Judge B. Fore.

Iwannit Now tries to make us want things that aren't good for us and not want things that are good. When he succeeds we make poor choices because our choices are influenced more by what we want than by what would be good for ourselves or others.

Biggs Bigger magnifies and exaggerates the importance or value of things. He blows things out of proportion and makes them seem bigger than they really are. Under his influence both desires and fears can loom so large we lose all perspective.

Eency Wency Tiny Too minimizes, discounts and undervalues things. He shrinks them out of proportion and makes them seem smaller than they really are. Generally when BB is around EWTT is there also. A thief overvalues money and undervalues the property rights of others. An addict overvalues pleasure and undervalues health.

Li Fib teaches us to intentionally deceive and mislead each other. Under her influence, it is nearly impossible to make sound choices. False information is a poor foundation for competent action. Deceit in any form is always a threat to thinking clearly.

Nameit Blameit uses labeling and blaming to confuse our thinking. Labeling is the use of a single word or phrase to express an idea. Blaming is fault finding and looking for weaknesses in others. Both are used to provide easy answers that have the goal of making people believe something without having to really think about it. Both inflame emotions and inhibit thought. Both appear to explain, yet tell you nothing. Both create conflict.

Judge B. Fore creates prejudice by getting us to make false assumptions. To prejudge a person or matter is to form an opinion prior to obtaining adequate information. Opinions so formed are nearly always contrary to the nature of things. Many foolish choices are made as the result of false assumptions and mistaken beliefs.

BEWARE THE STINK'N THINK'N GANG

ADVANCE PREPARATION: *Make photocopies of the gang members descriptions on pages 5 and 6 for each student in the class. Also photocopy the newscaster scripts below for each assigned newscaster. Assign three individuals to be newscasters and coach them on when to read their assigned scripts.*

Give descriptions of the Stink'n Think'n Gang to class members so they may follow along as newscaster #3 reads each description.

Newscaster Scripts

Newscaster 1:
Folks, I need to interrupt our regular programming for a breaking news story. Let's go to our reporter at the White House. (Name of newscaster 2), are you there?

Newscaster 2:
Yes, (name of newscaster 1). The president has just issued a warning that a vicious band of thieves named The Stink'n Think'n Gang is on the loose. Every citizen is at risk. No one is safe. If you are not careful, the Stink'n Think'n Gang will steal everything of importance to you. They will rob you of your ability to make good choices. First, they will steal your common sense and good judgment. They sneak in when you're not looking. They make you believe things that aren't true and want things that aren't good for you. They also make things seem more important or less important than they really are. If they succeed, they will rob you of your feelings of responsibility and fairness. They will steal your ability to be trustworthy and strip away your self-respect and respect for others. They will rob you of kindness and caring. They will even take away your desire to be a good person. Again, their goal is to rob you of your ability to think clearly and to make good choices. Now let's go to (name of newscaster #3) who has been following the situation.

Newscaster 3:
Thank you, (name of newscaster #2). We now have pictures of each member of the Stink'n Think'n Gang and their descriptions. I can also tell you something about how they operate and each gang member's specialty. Let me give you a rundown on each of these sinister characters. [Pass out the information sheets on the Stink'n Think'n Gang. Then read the information about each. Conclude with the following.] That's our rundown. Back to you, (newscaster 1.)

Newscaster 1:
There you have it folks. This is a mean bunch. Be on the look out for them. They will do you harm if you let them. Now back to our regular programming.

THE STINK'N THINK'N GANG
Your Worst Enemies

Iwannit Now – The leader of the Stink'n Think'n Gang tries to get you to make bad choices by influencing your wants. If he can get you to want things that are not good for you and not want things that are good, he can rob you of your ability to think clearly. Once Iwannit Now gets a good hold on you—Biggs Bigger, Li Fib and other members of the gang can pretty much get you to do most anything, no matter how foolish or hurtful it may be.

Biggs Bigger – Is like the mirror in the fun house that makes you look bigger than you really are. Biggs Bigger works closely with Iwannit Now. His job is to make you think things are more important, more valuable, more attractive, more desirable, more necessary, more urgent, and even more frightening than they really are. He tries to get you to blow things so far out of proportion you can no longer properly judge their true value or worth. In doing so he robs you of your ability to make good choices.

Eency Wency Tiny Too – Tries to make you think things are less important than they really are. He's like the fun house mirror that makes you look really small. He will try to make you think things are less less necessary, less desirable, less valuable, less urgent, less serious than they really are. He and Biggs Bigger work closely together. While Biggs tries to get you exaggerate the importance of one thing, Eency Wency tries to convince you something else is less important to you than it really is. For example, a thief thinks that what he wants is more important than what other people want. A drug user thinks pleasure is more important than health. Iwannit Now, Biggs Bigger and Eency Weency Tiny Too are all involved in these kinds of thinking.

Li Fib – Tries to make you believe things that aren't true. She will try to get you to lie to others and others to lie to you so neither of you know what to believe or do. She's at her best when she gets you to lie to yourself. She is most successful when she can get you to justify doing things you know are wrong or to believe things that will hurt you.

Nameit Blameit – Tries to make you think something is better or worse than it really is by how it is named. Nameit Blameit will try to get you to put labels on people or ideas and make you believe that if you know the name, you know the person or understand the idea. He uses names to make friends seem like enemies and enemies seem like friends. If you let him, he will make it nearly impossible for you to think clearly.

Judge B. Fore – Works closely with Nameit Blameit. He tries to get you to judge the worth of things before you know much about them. He will encourage you to form strong opinions with little or no information. His goal is to convince you that you are qualified to judge the value of a person or thing without making any real effort to know much about them.

Hindsight Questions
*   What does the Stink'n Think'n Gang want to take from you?
*   Who do you think is the leader of the gang?

Insight Questions
*   Why do you suppose Iwannit Now is the leader of the Stink'n Think'n Gang?
*   Why are these six thinking habits so dangerous?
*   Have you had any experiences with any of these thinking habits?

Foresight Questions
*   Why do you want to avoid these forms of thinking?
*   What can you do to avoid being influenced by the Stink'n Think'n Gang?

Discussion Opportunity: Explain that the Stink'n Think'n Gang wants to rob people of their ability to think clearly and make good choices. Iwannit Now may be considered the leader of the gang. When someone really wants something, it is easier for them to exaggerate the advantages and minimize the disadvantages of having it. It is easier for them to lie and to say mean things about others. It is easier for them to form judgments without getting all the facts and easier to make choices based on faulty thinking. Introduce the idea that to avoid faulty thinking, it is necessary to develop several thinking skills. Since faulty thinking almost always leads to poor choices, developing one's thinking skills is one of the most important things a person can do. Character Traits: PR ownership

---

ACTIVITY 2

BELIEVING IMPOSSIBLE THINGS

The queen remarked. . . .Now I'll give you something to believe. I'm just one hundred and one, five months, and a day."

"I can't believe that!" said Alice.

"Can't you?" the Queen said in a pitying tone. "Try again; draw a long breath, and shut your eyes."

Alice laughed. "There's no use trying," she said; "one can't believe impossible things."

"I dare say you haven't had much practice," said the Queen. "When I was your age I always did it for half an hour a day. Why, sometimes I've believed as many as six impossible things before breakfast."

From *Through the Looking Glass* by Lewis Carrol

Discussion Opportunity: Ask: Is it possible to believe impossible things? When you were little, what were some impossible things you believed? Do grownups ever believe impossible things? When people don't tell the truth (Li Fib), when they form opinions without correct information (Judge B. Fore) or when they exaggerate or minimize the importance of things (BB & EWTT), it becomes easy to believe impossible things. Character Traits: PR duty; T honesty.

ACTIVITY 3

GARBAGE IN—GARBAGE OUT

3-1 _____ Making Diamonds from Garbage _____

ADVANCE PREPARATION: *Assemble a pile of garbage and place it on a table in front of the classroom. At the appropriate time, explain that you wish to conduct an experiment and would like some help. Invite two students to come forward. Have one hold a plastic garbage bag while the other places the garbage in the bag.*

Tell your students that you have recently learned of a new method for creating diamonds out of ordinary garbage and that you wish to demonstrate the method for them. Ceremoniously tie the top of the bag so the garbage is securely enclosed. Then vigorously shake the bag so the contents get mixed around as much as possible.

When you have finished, ask your students what they think is in the bag. Invite the two students to open the bag and pour the contents back on the table so everyone can see whether they were right.

Hindsight Questions
• Why did you not believe that I could turn the garbage into diamonds?

Insight Questions
• How is this garbage bag like your mind?
• What do you think the term "garbage in—garbage out" means?
• Why is it important to be careful what you put into your mind?

Foresight Questions
• What kinds of ideas and information do you think would be good to put into your mind?
• What are some ways you can control the ideas and information that go into your mind?

Discussion Opportunity: "Making Diamonds from Garbage" is a fun way to demonstrate an important principle most people know but don't often think about. The principle is simply this—what we put into our minds will in large measure determine what we can get out. If you want to be a doctor, you have to put into your mind the things a doctor needs to know. This must be a conscious choice, it doesn't happen by chance. The same is true in every aspect of life. If we want to be mentally and emotionally healthy, there are some things we must choose to put into our minds and some things we must choose to keep out. It isn't always easy, but as the gate keepers of own minds we must take ownership of what goes in and what comes out. (See The Lesson of the Secret Garden on page 86.) Character Traits: PR ownership, accountability

---

3-2   Poor Little Plant

Obtain a small inexpensive plant. In front of class pour some turpentine or gasoline in the soil. Observe what happens to the plant over the next few days. What happens? Why?

3-3   Onion-Flavored Apple

Place apple slices in a closed container with raw onion slices. Leave over night. Invite students to smell and taste the apple slices. Which had the greater influence, the apple or the onions?

3-4   Brain Food

On a chalkboard or white board, or on a piece of paper, draw an outline of the human brain. Invite your students to identify some things they could take into their minds that might be considered garbage. Draw lines from the brain and write down the things they suggest. After listing several items, ask them to tell you what putting these thoughts or images in their minds might cause them to want to do. How is this an example of garbage in and garbage out?

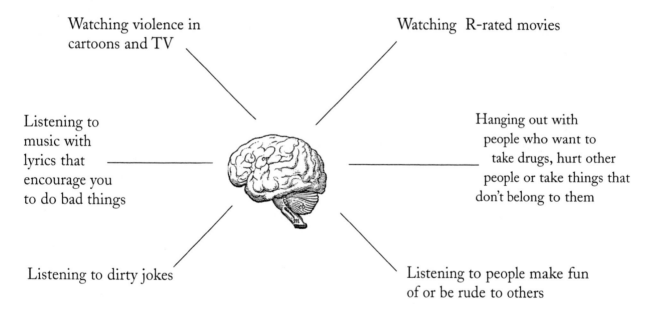

Watching violence in cartoons and TV

Watching R-rated movies

Listening to music with lyrics that encourage you to do bad things

Hanging out with people who want to take drugs, hurt other people or take things that don't belong to them

Listening to dirty jokes

Listening to people make fun of or be rude to others

Discussion Opportunity: To avoid being influenced by the Stink'n Think'n Gang, you have to avoid being in places where they hang out. You have to avoid reading literature they produce or watching movies they make. You have to avoid associating with people who are their accomplices. When you hang around people who lie, it becomes easy to do the same. If you frequently expose your mind to movies, magazines, or music that contain sex or violence, those are the things you will think about. Your mind is impressionable and picks up the knowledge, the thinking habits, the ideas you choose to feed it. Just like the body, the mind needs nutrition. It needs to be fed mental food that is healthy and that will improve your ability to think clearly. (See Charles Darwin quote on page 41.) Character Traits: PR ownership, accountability

ACTIVITY 4

THE PROBLEM WITH STINK'N THINK'N

ADVANCED PREPARATION: *Photocopy the activity sheet on page 11 for students to complete. After they have completed the activity, review their answers with them and discuss their thoughts about how each of these thinking habits can cause problems if we don't guard against them.*

Hindsight Questions
- What did you learn from this experience?

Insight Questions
- What is the flaw in this kind of thinking? (refer to a specific thought on the worksheet)
- Who does this kind of thinking hurt?
- Why is flawed thinking likely to cause problems for those affected by it?

Foresight Questions
- Why is it important to be aware of different kinds of flawed thinking?
- What can you do to be more aware of flawed thinking in yourself and others?

Discussion Opportunity: Invite your students to identify examples of flawed thinking they most frequently encounter and some of the problems they see resulting from it. Help them recognize problems that can arise when two people want the same thing, or when people want things that don't belong to them. When people get in this way of thinking they say and do things that are disrespectful to others and are sometimes even dishonest. If Iwannit Now can make you want something and Biggs Bigger makes it seem so important nothing else matters, then Eency Wency Tiny Too can step in and make other people and their feelings seem unimportant.

Similarly, if Judge B. Fore can convince a person that he or she is better than someone else, or worse than someone else, then Biggs Bigger can exaggerate the qualities of the person thought to be better and minimize the qualities of the person thought to be worse.

Judge B. Fore can also lead us to put our trust in people who can't be trusted or in ideas that won't stand up under investigation. The Stink'n Think'n Gang have many ways to get at us and we have to be on guard against them all the time. Character Traits: PR ownership; T honesty, dependability

---

The Problem With Stink'n Think'n

In each section, draw a line from the two thoughts to the problem each will likely cause

Thought	**Problem With the Thought**

Iwannit Now

"I want one of those sooo bad."

"Give it to me. It's my turn."

Cause a fight

Pay more than it's worth

Biggs Bigger

"Playing basketball in more important than anything."

"Their team is so good we don't stand a chance."

Give up too easy

Careless in other things

Eency Wency Tiny Too

"I don't need to know how to spell."

"No one likes me."

Limit opportunities

Feel sorry for self

Li Fib

"No one will know."

"If I say I am only eleven, I can get in free."

Loss of freedom and self-respect

Unable to recognize truth

Nameit Blameit

"You're a chicken. Show us how to cluck."

"Myrtle's a Turtle."

Causes hurt feelings

Creates anger and causes fights

Judge B. Fore

"I won't eat green eggs and ham."

"He walks and talks funny."

Unable to see other qualities

Unwilling to try new things

ACTIVITY 5

THE "I WANT" BIAS

5-1 _____ The Cookie Tin

ADVANCE PREPARATION: *Obtain a round tin container with a lid like those often used for fruit cakes or holiday cookies. Remove the lid and lay the container on its side. On the outside bottom of the tin container near the curvature on which* **Bottom**   **Inside**

the tin is resting, tape a small piece of paper with the words "I Want". On the inside bottom of the curvature, and opposite the "I Want" sign, tape a metal weight such as a heavy bolt or a nut. Replace the lid, lay the tin on its side again and gently roll it on a flat surface. The tin will roll forward, then stall and begin to rock back and forth until it comes to rest with the curvature where the "I Want" sign and the metal weight are on the bottom. As many times as you roll it, the tin will always come to rest in the same place.

Discussion Opportunity: This "cake" or "cookie" tin has a metal weight inside of it that causes it to always stop in the same place no matter how many times you roll it, or which direction you roll it. This is often how our minds work when we want something. Our thoughts always seem to come to rest on arguments in favor of getting or doing what we want and on arguments against getting or doing things we don't want. This is the goal of Iwannit Now. He wants us to only think about what we want—not about what someone else may want, not about whether it would be good for us—just about what we want. Character Traits: PR ownership; SR self-understanding; T honesty w/self

---

5-2 _____ One-Foot Balance _____

Have a student stand on one foot with arms outstretched. Hand the student a heavy object to put in one hand and it will pull him or her off balance.

Discussion Opportunity: Just like (the student) was pulled off balance when the (object) was placed in his/her hand, our wants can pull us off balance when making choices. When we want something we are more likely to choose it than if we don't want it. The more we want something, the more we are willing to pay for it or do to get it. If we want something very much we may think we cannot be happy without it. When this becomes a way of thinking, all of our thoughts seem to focus on how to get what we want. This kind of thinking can get us mentally and emotionally off balance and lead us to do foolish things. Character Traits: PR ownership; SR self-understanding; T honesty w/self

---

5-3 ————————— What do Smokers Want? —————————

Have your students place a hand over their mouth so that the thumb and forefinger of the hand block the nasal passages. Now ask them to breathe with their hands in this position for a moment. They will find that it is difficult to inhale and exhale and becomes extremely uncomfortable.
Ask: How did this make you feel?
         How would you feel if you had to breath like this all the time?
         Have you ever seen someone with an oxygen tank to help them breathe? Tell about it.

Explain that this is how people with a disease called emphysema feel. Emphysema affects the lungs and makes it difficult to breathe. Emphysema is one of the diseases that can be caused by smoking.

Now have your students spin around quickly several times while standing in place so they get a little dizzy. Have them sit down and ask: How did this make you feel?

Explain that this is how most people feel the first few times they smoke. Now ask:
    Since dizziness and nausea are not pleasant feelings for most people; why would a person smoke
       more than one cigarette? What is it they want?
    Since cigarette smoking can cause emphysema, why do people smoke? What do they want?

> **Discussion Opportunity:** This is an example of of Biggs Bigger and Eency Wency Tiny Too at work. Iwannit Now makes you want to feel cool and grown up. Biggs Bigger tries to make you think smoking will make you feel bigger and more important, even more powerful. Eency Wency Tiny Too will try to diminish the importance of feeling sick, even though the dizziness and nausea are nature's way of telling you cigarettes aren't good for you. When you get used to smoking Biggs will try to convince you the pleasure is worth more than the cost—even though the cost may eventually be emphysema. If BB and EWTT can influence you to think smoking is so cool and grown up that you are willing to get sick doing it and not worry about your health, they have succeeded. Character Traits: PR ownership; SR self-understanding, self-denial; T honesty, dependability

5-4 ————————— What Do Bullies Want —————————

Have your students number a piece of paper from 1 to 12. Explain that you are going to read twelve words. If they think a given word goes with the word "bully" they are to put a "Y" by the number. If they do not think the word goes with "bully" they are to put a "N" by the number. The twelve words are: 1) gentle, 2) caring, 3) tough, 4) secure, 5) loved, 6) mean, 7) unsafe, 8) big, 9) empty, 10) full, 11) comfortable, and 12) troubled.
After reading the words, write them on the board and get a count of how many answered yes and how many answered no to each word. Afterward, explore the following:

- Is the bully not loved because he is mean or is he mean because he doesn't feel loved? Why?
- Is the bully mean because he feels secure or because he feels insecure? Why?
- What does the bully want? What does he really need?
- What is Biggs Bigger telling the bully?
- What is Eency Wency Tiny Too telling the bully?
- Will bullying really give the bully what he wants?

Discussion Opportunity: Sometimes when people don't feel good about themselves, they try to build themselves up by tearing other people down. This is often the case when people are mean to each other. Teasing, picking on, name calling, pushing around, and even hitting on others are things bullies do. But they always do it to people they think are weaker than they are. To pick on others you think are weaker than you are is a mark of cowardice, not bravery. Biggs Bigger convinces the bully he will be bigger, more significant as a person, when he pushes others around. Eency Wency Tiny Too convinces him their feelings don't matter. They fail to realize that it is contrary to nature for people to feel better about themselves by tearing others down. Destructive behaviors may seem to generate temporary satisfactions, but they are not long lasting and can never generate self-respect. Character Traits: PR right, ownership; SR self-understanding, self-denial; T honesty, dependability

ACTIVITY 6

SELF-TALK

ADVANCE PREPARATION: *Invite a student to help you record the following script onto an audio tape.*

Teacher:	In class we have been learning about thinking. . .
Student:	I think Skooter, my new puppy is really cute. I can't wait to get home to see him.
Teacher:	. . .ability to think makes people different than animals like dogs or cats or . . . .
Student:	Can Skooter think? He can't talk. What can he think? Do monkeys really think?
Teacher:	. . . .than you could when you were younger.
Student:	Skooter's really young. Maybe mom will let me bring him for show and tell next week.
Teacher:	. . . .like running and jumping or to play a piano or. . . .
Student:	Dogs can't play a piano, but I can teach Skooter to run and jump. That will be fun.

Begin the activity by reading the following.

In class, we have been learning about thinking. Can you imagine what life would be like if you couldn't think. What could you do? What could you become? How does the ability to think make people different from cats or dogs or other animals? Just as you can do more things now than you could when you were younger, you can do more things than animals. But, just like any other skill, the ability to think takes effort to fully develop.

Explain that while you have been talking to them, they have also been talking to themselves. Play the tape recording as an example of self-talk. Being aware of our self-talk helps us be aware of our thinking.
- What was the teacher talking about?
- What was the student thinking and talking about?

Discussion Opportunity: A good clue as to what we consider important is what we spend most of our time thinking about. The ability to be aware of what you are saying to yourself will give you a good idea of whether the Stink'n Think'n Gang is working on you. Character Traits: PR ownership

ACTIVITY 7

THE STRANGE SAD TALE OF THE I-ME

by George L. Rogers

Not so long ago, and not so far away, there lived a strange creature called the I-Me. He lived in a land populated by a race of little furry creatures known as Thems. His parents were Thems and when he was born, he was cute and cuddly like other baby Thems. At first the I-Me seemed much like any other Them; he looked like they looked, he ate what they ate, and he played what they played. But as the I-Me began to grow, there was a strangeness about him that made him different from other Thems.

The I-Me's strangeness resulted from the fact that while he wanted very much to be happy, almost everything he did had the opposite effect. Indeed, to those around him, the I-Me often seemed to be the most unhappy creature they had ever seen. This was truly most strange, for everything the I-Me undertook to do was for the sole purpose of making himself happy. Now, you may ask, "How can this be?" I cannot say. I can only tell you his sad story and you will have to decide.

When the I-Me was very young, he somehow got the idea that to be happy he needed to always get or do just what he wanted. On the other hand, he thought having to do something he did not want to do, or not getting something that he wanted, could only make him unhappy. Well, this idea became so fixed in the I-Me's thinking, that no other possibilities for happiness ever entered his mind. Indeed, all the I-Me ever thought about was how to get what he wanted.

As he began to grow, this cute, cuddly, furry little creature began to have some rather uncuddly kinds of thoughts. The I-Me would think such things as "I want a Mega Monster video game. If I don't get one I'll be miserable." "I don't want to go to bed and if I have to go now, I will be very unhappy." "I want to go to the store with mom and if she won't take me, I will really be upset."

Now, like you and I, in one way or another, whatever the I-Me thought, he generally did. So when the I-Me did not get what he wanted, he felt it was necessary to demonstrate how truly unhappy he really was. So, the I-Me would release a torrent of tears, accompanied with a profusion of, "Why can't I's?," "I don't want to's," "You can't make me's," "Give it to me's," and "Please, please, please, I really want to's," with some "I hate you's" thrown in for good measure. There was no question. The I-Me was right. When he did not get what he wanted or when he had to do something he did not want to do, he was definitely unhappy. Now, like you and I, the I-Me frequently did not get what he wanted, and often had to do things he did not want to do, so you can see that from this cause alone, he was often very miserable.

Well, you must think as I did, that at least the I-Me was happy the rest of the time, certainly on those occasions when he did get his way. But, this was not true. Even when the I-Me got what he wanted, he was frequently disappointed. When he finally got the Mega Monster video game, it was broken within the hour. When he did get to stay up instead of going to bed, he usually became tired and cranky and spent most of his time arguing with his brothers and sisters. When he went to the store with his mom, he would constantly fuss because she would not buy him just what he wanted.

Even with his friends, while he still had some, the I-Me was no different. What he wanted was always more important than what they wanted, and he was never happy unless he got his way. Well, of course, not many little Thems were willing to play on those terms, so the I-Me was often alone and lonely.

So life went on for the I-Me, nothing ever working out quite like he expected. Whenever he ate all that he wanted, he got sick. Whenever he played as long as he wanted, he got too tired. Whenever he spent all of his money on one thing he wanted, he had to go without something else. Whenever he was in one place he always wanted to be someplace else. Things were always different for the I-Me than he expected and never quite what he wanted.

Well, like humans, Them's eventually grow old and leave this world. So did the I-Me. Whether he was richer for having lived, you will have to say.

Hindsight Questions
- Why was the I-Me so unhappy?
- Without naming names, have you ever seen anyone act like the I-Me, or have you ever acted like the I-Me?
- How happy did that person seem to you?
- How happy were you?

Insight Questions
- Why was the I-Me not more happy when he got what he wanted?
- How could thinking of others have helped the I-Me be more happy?

Foresight Questions
- What can you learn from the story of the I-Me?
- Why is it important to appreciate the things you have?
- Why is it important to take care of things you own?

Discussion Opportunity: Iwannit Now got an early hold on the the I-Me and never let go. The I-Me never seemed to recognize that thinking only of his own wants and never of others actually made him more miserable than happy. Therefore, he never had friends. Biggs Bigger convinced him that what he didn't have was more important and valuable than what he did have. Eency Wency Tiny Too even convinced him the things he did own were not worth taking care of, so they never worked long enough for him to get any real pleasure from having them. Character Traits: PR accountability; SR self-denial; RO caring, fairness

---

ACTIVITY 8

SNOW WHITE OPTICAL ILLUSION

ADVANCE PREPARATION: *Photocopy the optical illusion and coloring picture of Snow White on page 18. Other items needed by students are crayons and a 3 x 5 card.*

After reading and discussing "Snow White Wants It Now," use the optical illusion to further consider the illusionary relationship between satisfying wants and obtaining happiness.

ACTIVITY 9

SNOW WHITE WANTS IT ALL

The Brothers Grimm Fairy Tale *Snow White* Retold

True, it was once upon a time, and yes, it was long ago, but what matters, really, is the lesson it provides to all those whose wants exceed their wisdom.

A princess was born and the queen's wishes were granted. The child's skin was white as snow, her lips were red as blood, and her hair was black as ebony. The child was named Snow White. Year by year the child grew more and more lovely until, unquestionably, she became the fairest creature in all the land.

Unfortunately, her mother died shortly after her birth and the king took a new wife. The new queen was very beautiful, but alas, she was also very vain and proud. If you can imagine, each day she stood in front of a magic mirror and inquired:

Mirror, Mirror, on the wall
Who is the fairest of us all?

And the faithful mirror would answer,

You, my queen, are the fairest of them all.

Then, satisfied she was the most beautiful creature there ever was, the queen would go about her business for the day. That is, until one fateful day when her mirror responded:

Queen, you are full fair, tis verily true
But now Snow White is more fair than you.

Suddenly, filled with jealousy and hate, the queen's features, which only moments before had been most lovely to behold, were now dark and forbidding. For weeks the queen knew no peace as an evil plan formed in her mind. Snow White must die. To perform this foul deed she hired a

huntsman. He was to take Snow White into the woods, kill her, and bring back proof she was dead. Fortunately for Snow White, the huntsman, being a man of tender heart, was unable to slay the sweet and innocent child. Instead, he left Snow White unharmed in the woods and took the heart of a boar back to the queen as proof he had done as she had wished.

Frightened, and unsure what to do, Snow White wandered in the woods until she happened upon a small cottage in which there lived seven dwarfs. On hearing her sad story, the kindly dwarfs took the young girl in, fed her and gave her a place to sleep. Before leaving for work the next morning, the dwarfs warned Snow White to beware of strangers. You see, they had become very fond of Snow White and feared the queen would still try to harm her.

They were right, for at that very moment, the queen was standing before her mirror and asking,

Mirror, mirror on the wall,
Who is the fairest of us all?

Imagine, if you will, the queen's anger when she heard the mirror say,

Queen, thou art truly of beauty rare,
But Snow White who is living in the glen
With the seven little men
Is a thousand times more fair.

Knowing she had been deceived by the huntsman, the queen decided she must do the job herself. Dressed as an old peddler woman, the queen went to the glen and persuaded Snow White to buy some pretty lace. Then with a quickness that betrayed her age, the old woman quickly laced it around Snow White so tightly she could not

SNOW WHITE

OPTICAL ILLUSION AND COLORING PICTURE

Snow White Optical Illusion and Coloring Picture

Color the picture of Snow White and then watch the wicked queen hand Snow White the apple. To see Snow White take the apple from the wicked queen, place a 3 x 5 card on edge between Snow White's hand and the queen's hand. With both eyes open, lower your head so you can see Snow White with your left eye and the wicked queen with your right eye and see what happens.

breathe. Snow White would have died had the dwarfs not returned home in time to save her.

The next day, her little friends warned her again to beware of strangers, and the warning was needed. For, upon learning from her mirror that Snow White was still alive, the queen disguised herself again as an ugly old woman and returned to the glen. This time the wicked queen was selling beautiful combs with poison in them. Snow White thought, "Surely this old woman means no harm, and her combs are so lovely, I must have one." So she chose the comb she liked most, put it in her hair and fell immediately to the ground. The poor girl surely would have died, but fortunately, the dwarfs returned home again, just in time to save Snow White.

Greatly worried for their young friend, the dwarfs gave her a very stern warning before leaving for work the next day. "Do not trust anyone," they said. On learning her second attempt had failed, the queen resolved to try one more time. By now the wicked queen had become truly ugly. Jealousy and envy had so cankered her soul she was no longer beautiful at all. She knocked at the window chanting, "Apples for sale. Delicious, juicy apples for sale." Snow White hesitated, but an apple sounded so good, she could not resist the temptation and opened the window. Snow White almost shuddered when she saw the ugliness of the old woman, but the apples looked so red and

juicy, she felt she had to have one. Choosing to ignore her past experiences and the warnings of her friends, Snow White took the apple the old woman offered her. Unaware that the wicked queen had filled the apple with poison, Snow White bit into it and immediately fell dead.

For all her folly, Snow White led a charmed existence. Her dwarf friends placed her in a glass coffin that they placed on a pedestal in the glen. One day, a prince in passing by, was much taken by her beauty. After much effort, he persuaded the dwarfs to move the coffin to another location where he could look upon her more often. In moving the coffin, Snow White was jostled and choked up the piece of poisonous apple that had lodged in her throat. She sat up, now alive and well. Overcome with joy, the prince took her with him to be his wife.

The wicked queen was not so fortunate. Thinking Snow White dead, the queen returned to her magic mirror to admire her own beauty and to ask her favorite question. But, when the queen looked in the mirror and saw that she was no longer beautiful, but instead had become a most ugly creature, she ran from the castle and threw herself into a nearby lake. Rumor has it that upon throwing herself into the lake, all the fish therein jumped out. They refused to live there any longer, declaring it an unfit place for any self-respecting fish. At least, so I have heard.

Hindsight Questions
* What did the queen want?
* What did the queen do?
* What happened as a result?

Insight Questions
* How did the queen's wants affect her ability to care about Snow White?
* What makes you think Snow White had trouble learning from experience?
* How did Snow White's wants influence her choices?

Foresight Questions
* How can you tell when your wants are getting out of hand? What are some clues?
* How can you recognize when things you want may not be good for you?

> **Discussion Opportunity:** Iwannit Now, a particularly vicious member of the Stink'n Think'n Gang took hold of the queen's ability to think. She wanted to be the fairest woman in the land. Biggs Bigger convinced her it was more important than anything else. As a result she chose to disguise herself as an ugly old woman in an attempt to kill her own stepdaughter. This is an example of how Iwannit Now can twist a person's thinking so he or she makes foolish choices and does foolish things. Iwannit Now also got hold of Snow White. Under his influence and that of Biggs Bigger and Eency Wency Tiny Too, she wanted the lace, the comb and later the apple more than she wanted to listen to the warnings of her friends. Character Traits: PR right, accountability; SR self-denial; RO caring, T honesty

ACTIVITY 10

THE GOOSE THAT LAID EGGS OF GOLD

An Aesop Fable Retold

Listen up m'lads and lassies,
As I tell a tale of woe,
Now, you may wonder at it,
I doubt myself t'was ever so.

But, the lesson, my young'uns,
Aye, tis the lesson,
That makes it worth the telling,
And worth your while to listen.

For as the story goes,
In days of old,
There once was a goose,
That laid eggs of gold.

And though her master,
Wasn't exactly what you'd call wealthy,
He had many reasons,
To keep this bird healthy.

For the golden eggs,
He was able to sell,
Enabled him to live,
Extremely well.

But, not being wealthy,
Made him feel poor,
And one day he wished,
For just another egg more.

Just one more egg,
That was what he thought,
For with a single egg,
A lot could be bought.

But this one little idea,
When it entered his brain,
Lit it on fire,
And set it aflame.

"Oh! No! No! That's not enough,"
Thought he,
"To get what I want,
I'll need two dozen, no, three!"

"Three? Three dozen?
Yes, three will do!
And if worst comes to worst,
I can get by with two."

For he truly imagined,
In a mind, troubled, and unsound,
That within his poor goose,
Three dozen gold eggs could be found.

It never, ever occurred to him,
That stacked together on a shelf,
Only eight or ten of those eggs,
Would be larger than the goose herself.

But in his fantasy world,
It seemed ever so real,
And so the fate of his goose,
His fantasy did seal.

For the terrible plan,
That now formed in his mind,
Was to cut open his goose,
To get all the eggs he could find.

Of course, to do this,
The poor bird had to die,
So, with a little grain in his hand,
He coaxed her to come nigh.

And, as many an innocent,
She trusted her master,
Never, ever, suspecting,
Her impending disaster.

Then suddenly without warning,
Before she could run,
He quickly pounced upon her,
And, in an instant, the deed was done.

But, when he opened up his goose,
And reached down inside,
Fear clutched at his heart,
And in panic he cried.

"There are no eggs! no eggs!,
Not one egg to be found!"
And groaning in misery,
He fell to the ground.

For he saw all at once,
That he'd been woefully deceived.
In all that he hoped,
And all that he believed,

And that he had destroyed
By his very own hand,
The source of his wealth,
And any happiness he'd planned.

So, my young friends,
If something you want or think you may need,
Is ever influenced,
By even the faintest of greed.

Just remember this tale,
From days of old,
And the fate of the goose,
That laid eggs of gold.

And how her master,
Let his passions run loose,
And by his own hands,
Cooked his own goose.

Hindsight Questions
- Why did the man kill his goose?

Insight Questions
- What did the man want? What did he get?
- How was he influenced by Iwannit Now, Biggs Bigger and Eency Weency Tiny Too?

Foresight Questions
- Why do we need to be careful what we want?

Discussion Opportunity: In his greed, fostered by Iwannit Now and Biggs Bigger, this man killed his very means of livelihood. In real life, people do the same thing. A young man who gives in to drugs and can no longer perform effectively in school is one example. Another is a young girl who ends up in reform school for stealing a car. Most things of worth require some degree of patience and effort to acquire them. Character Traits: PR accountability; SR self-denial

---

ACTIVITY 11

IT'S ALL IN THE MIND

ADVANCE PREPARATION: *Draw these faces on the board.*
Read the story below and ask your students to identify the person that goes with each face and tell you how each is being influenced by Biggs Bigger and/or Eency Wency Tiny Too.

Mrs. Maxfield said, "Alright children, it is time for show and tell."
Amy smiled and said, "No one can beat what I brought today, peanut butter cookies." (2)
Freddie frowned and grumbled to himself, "I hate show and tell time. It's so boring." (6)
Natalie thought, "Humph! My show and tell is much better than Amy's cookies." (3)
"Yum!" thought Ahmad. "I really like peanut butter cookies. I could eat a million of them" (5)
Reuben thought, "Yuk! I hate peanut butter cookies. I wish they had never been invented." (8)
Tommy was worried. "I can't get up in front of everybody. They will think I'm stupid." (7)
Milo was quite bashful, (1) but when it was his turn he slowly walked to the front of the class carrying a canvas bag. When he reached Mrs. Maxfield's desk, he reached into his bag and pulled out a small, green, wiggly thing and put it on her desk. Mrs. Maxfield let out a scream. (4) Milo said, "Don't worry Mrs. Maxfield. It's just a little garter snake. It won't hurt anyone."

Discussion Opportunity: Amy (2) and Natalie (3) thought they were in competition. They exaggerated their own contributions and undervalued the contributions of others. Freddie (6) devalued the whole experience and refused to learn from it. Ahmad (5) exaggerated how many cookies he could eat and would probably get sick if he ate all he wanted. Reuben (8) devalued Amy's cookies. Tommy (7) undervalued himself and what he had to show and tell. Milo (1) was bashful. He too, undervalued himself and felt insecure around others. Mrs. Maxfield (4) overreacted by exaggerating the dangerous nature of the snake. When we undervalue others we lack respect for them. When we undervalue ourselves we lack self-respect. One of the great challenges in life is to learn to properly value things. Character Traits: PR ownership; SR self-understanding, RO caring

---

ACTIVITY 12

THE DOG WITHOUT A BONE

An Aesop Fable Retold

The dog with the bone,
Was on his way home,
Wagging his tail,
As he followed the trail.

Up over the ridge,
And down to the bridge,
Where the waters cool,
Formed a great big pool.

Humming a song,
And as he walked along,
For the sun was bright,
And his heart was light.

"Oh Fiddle dee-dee,
Oh happy is me,
I found me a bone,
And it's all my own."

He came round the bend
To the bridges end,
Gave his head a toss,
Then started across.

When out of his eye,
He happened to spy,
A little green frog,
Just sitting on a log.

Then startled was he,
To suddenly see,
The face of a dog,
In the water by the log.

A dog with a bone,
Just like his own,
Looking up at him,
With a very silly grin.

Then filled with greed,
For he had no need,
He wanted that bone,
As well as his own.

So standing on a beam,
He hatched a scheme,
To frighten that dog,
In the water by the log.

Bark went the dog,
Hop went the frog,
Plop by the log,
Fell the bone from the dog.

He gave a groan,
A great big moan,
For where that bone,
Had fallen like a stone.

He saw a fool,
Just sitting in the pool,
Looking up at him,
From the waters dim.

A dog without a bone,
To call his own,
A dog without a grin,
And that dog was him.

So he started on home,
Without his bone,
Just dragging his tail,
Along the trail.

Hindsight Questions
- How did the dog lose his bone?

Insight Questions
- What did the dog overvalue?
- What did he undervalue?

Foresight Questions
- What can you learn from this story?

Discussion Opportunity: The dog wanted two bones, not just one. In fact, he wanted the second bone so much he was willing to take it from the other dog. Biggs Bigger convinced him that it was more important for him to have the bone than for the other dog to have it. Eency Wency Tiny Too convinced him the other dog's rights and feelings didn't matter. So limited was his thinking, the possibility of losing his own bone never even occurred to him. Character Traits: RO accountability; SR self-denial; RO care, citizenship

ACTIVITY 13

WHEN THE HARE WOKE UP

An Aesop Fable Retold

For a thousand years, the story's been told,
Of the tortoise and the hare,
And the lessons learned from the race between,
This most unlikely pair.

It all began when the hare was boasting,
As animals sometimes do,
That among all the critters of the field,
He was the fastest one he knew.

Said the hare, pointing to a big elm tree,
"I'll race from here to there,
Any creature who thinks it's faster
Than this humble little hare."

The tortoise, when no one else came forward,
Stepped up to the line.
"Meet me here tomorrow," said the tortoise,
"We'll start the race at nine."

The air was crisp, the sun was bright,
The day was clear and fair.
Spectators had come from far and near,
To see the tortoise race the hare.

No one doubted the hare would win,
For the tortoise was mighty slow,
But the tortoise was determined,
While the hare was mostly show.

The two met at the starting line,
Excitement filled the air,
A shot was fired and the race was on,
Between the tortoise and the hare.

The hare raced off, but soon was back,
To wave the tortoise on,
He jeered and teased that poor old tortoise,
But the tortoise plodded on.

Again, the hare raced out of sight
Then quick as he was gone,
The hare was back to laugh and mock,
But the tortoise plodded on.

Then the hare laid down as if to nap,
And gave a mighty yawn.
He stretched and yawned and stretched again,
As the tortoise plodded on.

Then what should happen but that silly hare,
Actually went to sleep,
While the tortoise kept on plodding,
Though his plod was but a creep.

Then just in time, the hare woke up,
To find he'd lost the race,
And to learn that steady progress,
Is more important than the pace.

Hindsight Questions

• What was important to the hare?

Insight Questions

• Why do you think this was important to the hare?
• How did this influence the hare's Choices?

Foresight Questions

• What qualities did the tortoise have?
• How can these same qualities help you?

Discussion Opportunity: The hare wanted to prove he was better than the other creatures in the field. Biggs Bigger encouraged him to think that his speed made him better and that speed was the only important quality in measuring betterness. Because the tortoise was slower, Eency Wency Tiny Too encouraged him to think the Tortoise was not as good as he. True the hare was faster, but in the end winning the race depended on qualities other than speed. When we start worrying about who's better than who, we may undervalue qualities others have and treat them disrespectfully. Character Traits: SR self-understanding

ACTIVITY 14

THE PRICE IS RIGHT

ADVANCE PREPARATION: *Bring to class a few items students are familiar with and may have some idea of what they cost. Write the price of each object on a 4 x 6 card. Place the items in front of the class so everyone can see what they are.*

Divide the class into small groups. Each group is to discuss and decide what they think the price of each item is and write the item and the amount on a piece of paper. Then have each group tell you the price they decided on for each item. Write their answers on the board.

After all the answers are written on the board, place the 4 x 6 card with the real price in front of each object. Compare their answers with the real cost to see which was the closest. Point out that when people spend money to buy any of these items, the item is worth more to them than the money they are spending to buy it. Ask and discuss:

- If people spend money to buy things, what do they have to spend to earn the money?
- What do people have to spend to develop the talents and skills they need to earn money?

Consider different ways in which people spend time, energy, and ability to get and do things they want. Point out that in each case, the person is exchanging one thing of value for something they feel is of greater value. Then explore the discussion points to be made for this section.

Hindsight Questions
- In buying and selling, which is most important to the seller, the money or the thing? To the buyer?

Insight Questions
- How does our choice of how we spend money show what we think is important?
- How does our choice of how we spend time show what we think is important?

Foresight Questions
- Why is it important to be thoughtful in how we spend time and money?

Discussion Opportunity: All people have the same amount of time. We choose to spend our share of it for those things we think are most important. Where we choose to spend our money and talents are also expressions of what we think is most important. If we want things that aren't good for us and Biggs Bigger convinces us we must have them—or if we don't want things that are good for us and Eency Wency Tiny Too convinces us they're not important—then we'll spend our time, money, and talents on things that are more likely to hurt than to help us. Character Traits: PR duty, accountability

ACTIVITY 15

O MAN OF THE SEA

Jakob and Wilhelm Grimm's *The Fisherman and His Wife* Retold

15-1 ————————————— The Plague of My Life ——————————

Once there was a poor fisherman who lived with his wife in a little dirt hut by the sea. One day the fisherman pulled a great fish out of the water. No sooner had he brought the fish ashore, than it spoke to him saying, "Pray let me live. I am not a real fish, but an enchanted prince."

The startled fisherman said, "I will have nothing to do with a fish that can talk." and quickly put the fish back in the water.

When the fisherman told his wife of the fish he had caught, she said, "Did you not ask it for any- thing?"

"No" said the man, "what should I have asked for?"

"What should you have asked for?" exclaimed the wife, "We live miserably in a dirt hut by the sea. Go tell the fish we want a cottage."

The fisherman did not much like the idea, but he went back to the place where he had caught the fish. He stood on the shore and said:

> O man of the sea!
> Come listen to me,
> For Alice my wife,
> The plague of my life,
> Hath sent me to beg a boon of thee!

With that, the fish swam to him and said, "What does she want?"

"My wife says that when I let you go, I should have asked you for a cottage."

"Go!" said the fish, "she is in a cottage already."

The man quickly returned home to see his wife standing in the door of a pretty cottage where the dirt hut had been. Quite pleased he said, "Now we shall live together quite happily."

But after a few days, his wife said the cottage was too small and that she would be much happier living in a cas- tle. So, reluctantly he went back to the fish and plead,

> O man of the sea!
> Come listen to me,
> For Alice my wife,
> The plague of my life,
> Hath sent me to beg a boon of thee!

The great fish rose from the water and said, "What does she want?"

"A castle," said the fisherman.

"Go! She is in a castle now," the fish said and then swam away.

The fisherman was most pleased with their castle, but after awhile his wife was not content. Nothing would do but that he should be king and she should be queen. "Go tell the fish what I want," she demanded. The man did not like the idea but he did as she said. A third time he said:

> O man of the sea!
> Come listen to me,
> For Alice my wife,
> The plague of my life,
> Hath sent me to beg a boon of thee!

"What do you want now?" asked the great

fish swimming to him.

"My wife desires that we should be king and queen," said the man.

"Pooh! That is too much." said the fish. "Go back to your mud hut." With that the fish swam away and was never seen again.

The man returned home to find his wife in their old mud hut where they lived the rest of their lives.

Hindsight Questions
- What was important to the fisherman's wife?
- What was important to the fisherman?

Insight Questions
- Why will the fisherman's wife never be happy?
- Why did the fish send them back to the mud hut?
- Which members of the Stink'n Think'n Gang were working on the man's wife?

Foresight Questions
- What can you learn from this story?
- How can being thankful for what you have help you be happy?

Discussion Opportunity: Apparently the fish reasoned that if the fisherman's wife could not be pleased, it did not matter whether she lived in a castle or a mud hut. No matter what she had, she wanted more. She had fallen victim to Iwannit Now and his partners in crime, Biggs Bigger and Eency Wency Tiny Too. What she did have was always of less value than what she did not have. Character Traits: PR ownership, accountability; SR self-denial

---

15-2   The Plague of My life Activity Sheet

ADVANCE PREPARATION: *Photocopy the activity sheet on page 28 for each student.*

The activity sheet is designed to stimulate a discussion around the idea that people sometimes want things that are not good for them and, conversely sometimes don't want things that are good for them. It also provides an an opportunity to explore why happiness is not closely related to the possession of things.

Discussion Opportunity: Benjamin Franklin once wrote, "What is without us has not the least connection with happiness only so far as the preservation of our lives and health depends on it. . . .If our desires are to the things of this world, they are never to be satisfied. . . .There is no happiness but in a virtuous and self-approving conduct." *Benjamin Franklin's The Art of Virtue* p. 35. Iwannit Now will try to convince you differently. Biggs Bigger will try to help him. But think about things you have wanted and gotten and what real difference they made in your life. Character Traits: PR ownership; SR self-denial

---

The Fisherman and His Wife Activity Sheet

True or False?

____ The fisherman's wife was more happy living in the castle than she was in the cottage.

____ The fisherman's wife did not like the cottage because it was too small for their needs.

____ The fisherman and his wife would not have made a good king and queen because they thought only of what they wanted.

____ The fisherman's wife always wanted more than what she had.

____ The fisherman did not want to go ask the fish for what his wife wanted.

____ The fisherman wanted to please his wife more than he wanted to please the fish.

____ People who live in castles are always more happy than people who live in mud huts.

____ People always want things that are good for them.

____ People never want things that aren't good for them.

What did you learn from the story of "The Fisherman and His Wife"?

ACTIVITY 16

CRAZY COOTE

Author Unknown

"There's no question, Miss Coote's a shoplifter. She even has a prison record. I've heard it from several people."

The boys listened carefully to the conversation. They were eating birthday cake and ice cream as several of their mothers stood around the table talking. The boys were fascinated. Old Miss Coote was really a crook.

"Oh, I'm sure not...." one of the mothers started to say.

She was interrupted by another woman, "I don't think she's a thief, I think she's just plain crazy. I saw her out in her yard yesterday, in a feathered hat and white gloves teaching her dreadful dog to jump over a stick."

Miss Coote was an elderly spinster who lived in a neighborhood of young families. They all lived in modern, gaily painted homes. Her house was at least fifty years old. It was large and dark, surrounded by a picket fence. But her yard was neat and she kept a small garden. She had a mongrel dog named Red and a ginger cat. Miss Coote wore high button shoes to church and her clothes looked as old as her house. Whenever she went out, she carried a large black umbrella.

Actually, for the most part the women in her neighborhood thought Miss Coote was a sweet old lady, quiet and timid. It's just that she was the only different person in the neighborhood. They had gotten into the habit of gossiping about her, more in fun than anything. They would make up ridiculous stories and giggle about it. "Do you know, Miss Coote feeds her dog on T-bone steak?" one would say. Another would respond, "With the price of steak, she must be a shoplifter. I can just see her popping diamond rings into that big coat she wears." Then they would all laugh. After all, they were just having a little harmless fun. But now, it seemed, Miss Coote was not the innocent old woman they had thought she was.

The boys finished their cake and ice cream and went outside. It wasn't long before the mothers heard sticks banging on a picket fence and several boys chanting, "Crazy Coote! Crazy Coote!" They ran out just in time to see the boys throw their sticks at Miss Coote who was in her yard and hear them change their chant to, "Thief! Thief! Crazy Coote's a sneak thief!"

Miss Coote backed toward her house with tears streaming from her eyes. Just then, her dog Red jumped over the fence and attacked the boys. In the ruckus, one of the boys was badly bitten.

Now the neighborhood talk became. "Vicious old dog!" "Horrid old woman!" So strong was the community reaction that it was front page news that "Old Red" was to be destroyed. But, before that happened, Miss Coote's shades were drawn and her front door was padlocked. Miss Coote had gone away. Good riddance thought many.

But, there were some who realized that what had happened had more to do with something they had done than with what Miss Coote had done. Their innocent fun had not been so innocent after all.

Hindsight Questions
- What did the boys call Miss Coote?
- What else did they do?

Insight Questions
- How did the labels "thief" and "crazy" influence how the boys treated Miss Coote?
- Why was this unfair to Miss Coote?

Foresight Questions
- How would you feel if someone treated you like this neighborhood treated Miss Coote?
- How would you feel if you were the mother who wrote this story?

> **Discussion Opportunity:** Nameit Blameit had great success in this story. He succeeded in placing names on Miss Coote that blamed her for things she had never done. He even named her dog "horrid" and blamed it for attacking the boys. Nameit Blameit's greatest success comes when he can pit people against one another. Li Fib and Judge B. Fore were also at work. Can you tell where? Most labels are based on falsehoods and prejudice. Character Traits: PR right, accountability; RO caring, fairness; T honesty

ACTIVITY 17

WHO SHALL I BELIEVE?

Select three students. One is to be blindfolded. Explain to the three students and the rest of the class that the objective is for the blindfolded student to get from point A to point B in the classroom by following the instructions of the other two students, one of whom will be providing correct instructions. The other will be providing incorrect instructions. It is the blindfolded person's job to decide which person's instructions are the correct ones to follow. Blindfold and turn the student around a couple of times. Hand a note to each of the two students to inform them as to whether they will be providing the correct or incorrect instructions. Then tell them when to start and see what happens.

Hindsight Questions
- What happened in this/these activities?

Insight Questions
- What is the problem with wrong information/directions?
- Why do people give others wrong information/directions?

Foresight Questions
- How can you protect yourself from getting wrong information/directions?
- What do you need to do when you find out you have been given wrong information/directions?

> **Discussion Opportunity:** It is nearly impossible to go the right way or do the right thing when given wrong information or directions. Right action requires right information. There are many reasons people give wrong information. Sometimes they are simply mistaken. Other times it is deliberate. People who deliberately lie are dangerous—particularly if they are lying for personal gain. A person who will deceive someone else for personal gain, will deceive you if it seems to their advantage. Li Fib can convince people to do many hurtful things. Character Traits: T dependability, honesty

ACTIVITY 18

ADVERTISING AWARENESS ACTIVITIES

George Will wrote an article "Born to be Consumers" published in the May 6, 2001 edition of *The New York Times*. In the article, he talks about advertisers who target child consumers and the sophisticated behavioral studies they use to manipulate young people's attitudes. In the article, Will quoted one advertiser as saying, "Advertising at its best is making people feel that without their product you're a loser. Kids are very sensitive to that."

Use the following activities to examine various types of advertising to identify ways in which advertisers try to get people, and especially young people, hooked on their products. Have students look for ways the advertiser is trying to make them want the product, ways in which it presents people who use the product as winners and suggests that those who do not use the product may be losers. Also, have them look for other ways in which the advertisement may be stretching or even altering the truth.

18-1   Magazine Advertisements

Cut out full-page advertisements for a variety of consumer products and paste them on colored construction paper. Discuss the questions below.

18-2   Scrap Book

Assign students into small groups to find and cut out advertisements from newspapers and magazines. Have each group paste the ads in a scrapbook and make notes about each ad.

Hindsight Questions
- What does this advertiser want people to do?
- What do they do in the ad to make you want their product?

Insight Questions
- What did the advertiser do, if anything, to stretch the truth?
- What did the advertiser do, if anything, to associate the product with winners.

Foresight Questions
- Why is it an advantage to be able to recognize when advertisers are doing these things?

Discussion Opportunity: In an effort to persuade people to purchase their products, many advertisers attempt to create the impression that people who use their products are winners and those those who do not are losers. They use labels to do this. Did you recognize any? Another way they do this is by associating their products with famous people who are "winners." Almost all advertising is designed to make somebody want something. Character Traits: PR duty; T honesty, dependability

---

ACTIVITY 19

PINOCCHIO'S FIELD OF MIRACLES

Adapted from The Adventures of Pinocchio *by D. Collodi*

Geppetto loved Pinocchio and wanted him to learn to read and write. So he sold his coat to buy Pinocchio a spelling book and sent him off to school. On the way, Pinocchio passed a puppet show he greatly wanted to see. So he sold his spelling book and bought a ticket to the puppet show instead of going to school. After a sad adventure at the theater, in which he was almost put into a fire, the showman gave Pinocchio five gold pieces to take home to his father.

On his way home, Pinocchio noticed a Fox and a Cat begging on the street. He saw that the Fox was lame and the Cat was blind. As Pinocchio walked by, the Fox politely said, "Hello, Pinocchio. How are you today?"

Startled, Pinocchio stopped. "How do you know my name?" he asked.

"I know your father well," replied the Fox. "Just this morning I saw him shivering in the cold without a coat."

"My poor Papa!" exclaimed Pinocchio. "But soon he shall shiver no more." Pinocchio then told the Fox he had just been given five gold pieces and was on his way home to buy Geppetto a new coat.

"Pity you're in such a hurry," said the Fox. "For if you could wait until morning, you could give him much more than just five gold pieces."

"How is that?" asked Pinocchio. The Fox told Pinocchio about a Field of Miracles in which he could bury his five gold pieces and by morning the five would have grown to be as many as two thousand.(1)

This information greatly pleased Pinocchio. He began to imagine that by morning he could be a very rich puppet indeed.(2) So Pinocchio told the Fox that if he and the Cat would lead him to the Field of Miracles and show him what to do, he would give them five hundred of the 2,000 gold pieces for themselves.

"Oh no," said the Fox. "We do not do this for ourselves. We only wish to help you."

"Then let us go at once," said Pinocchio and with that the three began their journey.

They walked for a very long time, then as evening drew on they stopped to eat at the Inn of the Red Crawfish. After a good meal, they obtained a room in which to rest until midnight when they planned to continue their journey. When the innkeeper woke Pinocchio at midnight he informed him that the Fox and the Cat had gone on ahead, but they would meet him at the Field of Miracles.

Shortly after he started on his journey, the cricket from Geppetto's house stopped Pinocchio and warned him, "Do not trust those who promise to make you rich in a day. Beware and turn back."

But Pinocchio, his head filled with visions of gold pieces, ignored the cricket and continued on his way. (3) Before he had traveled far, he was aware of two black figures shadowing him in the dark. Suddenly the figures pounced upon him and demanded, "Your money or your life."

With a surprising show of strength, Pinocchio broke free and fled. But after a frightful race the robbers caught up with Pinocchio. In the heat of the battle, Pinocchio bit off the hand of one of his assailants. As he spit it out, he was surprised to discover that it was the paw of a cat.

Nevertheless, Pinocchio was the loser, and in the end, the two robbers overcame Pinocchio and hung him from the limb of an old oak tree. But, try as they might, they did not succeed in getting his five gold pieces.

As Pinocchio was dangling from the tree, a beautiful Fairy saw him bobbing in the air and sent a large Falcon to release Pinocchio and bring him to her home in the forest. Pinocchio was nearly dead, but the Fairy was a good nurse, and with the help of three doctors, a Crow, an Owl, and a Talking Cricket, she was able to get him back on his feet again. While caring for Pinocchio, the Fairy learned about his story from the Cricket who seemed to know Pinocchio very well. So she sent for Geppetto whom she knew would be very anxious to learn about his little puppet son.

Eager to see Geppetto again, Pinocchio set out to meet his dear father. Shortly after leaving the good Fairy's house, who should Pinocchio see but the Fox and the Cat. When they asked him why he had not come to the Field of Miracles, he told them of his battle with the robbers and how the Fairy had saved him. As they were talking, Pinocchio noticed the Cat was missing a paw and asked her how she lost it. The Fox, with a tear in his eye, explained that the Cat, out of the goodness of her heart, had bitten off her paw and given it to a hungry wolf who was starving. Pinocchio was very touched by this story of the Cat's generosity. (4)

"We must hurry!" said the Fox. "The Field of Miracles has been sold and after today no one will be allowed to bury money there."

Convinced he must hurry, Pinocchio went with the Fox and the Cat who showed him how and where to bury the money.

Hindsight Questions
- What did the fox and the cat want?
- What lies did the fox tell Pinocchio?
- What did Pinocchio want?

Insight Questions
- Why did Pinocchio believe the fox?
- Why was Pinocchio unwilling to believe the cricket who was really his friend?
- How was Pinocchio his own worst enemy?

Foresight Questions
- What could Pinocchio have done differently?
- What can you learn from Pinocchio?

Discussion Opportunity: 1) The Fox wanted Pinocchio's five gold pieces. Li Fib convinced the Fox the best way to get them would be to tell Pinocchio a lie. (2) Biggs Bigger magnified the benefits of being wealthy in Pinocchio's mind. Because the idea pleased Pinocchio, he believed the Fox. (3) Pinocchio's greed created an "I Want" bias so strong, he was unwilling to listen to the Cricket's warning. (4) The Fox continued to lie to Pinocchio. But, Iwannit Now and Biggs Bigger had such a hold on Pinocchio he was willing to believe anything the Fox told him. Eency Wency Tiny Too even caused him to forget his experience in bitting off the cat's paw. So, Pinocchio chose to ignore every piece of information that could tell him he was being deceived. Character Traits: PT duty, accountability; RO citizenship; T honesty, dependability

ACTIVITY 20

HE'S NO DUCK AT ALL

Hans Christian Anderson's *The Ugly Duckling* Retold

The mother duck felt a strong tapping underneath her. She stood up, and, sure enough, the egg she was sitting on was starting to crack open. Soon there was a hole big enough for the baby bird to crawl out. This egg was larger than her others had been, and it had taken much longer to hatch. She was not even sure the egg was her own. Nevertheless, she had patiently sat on it, keeping it warm until the baby duckling was ready to come out. But, the mother duck was not prepared for what she saw. This baby was nothing like her other ducklings. It was a large, gangling, awkward, clumsy thing with a plump gray body and a long neck. It even made different sounds than her other ducklings did. Nevertheless, her mothering instincts were strong, and she chose to take the baby in as one of her own.

Unfortunately, other ducks in the duck yard were not so kind. The older ducks criticized the mother as foolish and looked down on this new arrival as if it were something from another planet. The younger ducks called it names and made fun of it. Some even bullied it by chasing and pecking at it. But through it all, the mother duck stood by her little one, telling the others, "He may not look like much, but he swims well." and "He has a lot of spunk, I do believe he will amount to something."

To him she would say, "Pay them no mind. You may be different, but that doesn't mean they are any better than you." and, "Just pay no atten-tion to them, some day they will be ashamed they were so unkind to you."

Of course this was very difficult for the young bird. He often wondered why they didn't like him. He felt out of place and often wondered, "Am I really a duck? Perhaps I'm a turkey or a goose just like they say. I don't know, but I know that, for some reason, I am different than everyone else."

His mother would console him by saying, "Just be patient and do your best. In time all will come out. You are a fine swimmer and have many other qualities that will make you glad to be who you are."

But, for whatever reason, it was easier for the young duckling to believe the other ducks than his mother. "I am ugly," he said. "No wonder they don't like me."

Finally, he could take the teasing and bullying no longer. One fall day, he flew away with some wild geese that invited him to come with them. Eventually, they landed in a field to rest. No sooner had they landed than he heard two loud bangs. He turned and saw his two companions lying dead beside him. Terrified the young duck-ling ran into some brush and hid while a hunter came and picked up the two geese he had killed.

He waited for a while after the hunter left and then flew away, not knowing, or even caring, where he was going. He flew until he was too tired to go any farther, and then landed on a small pond. Feeling lost and very lonely the little duck-ling just swam around and around the pond, day after day, not knowing where else to go or what else to do. The weather was getting colder and soon winter set in. Gradually, the water turned into ice, and before he knew it, the little duckling was frozen in the pond and could not move. Fortunately, a man walking by saw the little bird stuck in the ice and broke him free.

Having pity on the poor bird, the man took him home to warm him up and feed him. Here, the duckling lived until spring with the man and his family, along with their cat and chickens.

Being neither a chicken nor a cat, which became obvious when he found he had no red comb and couldn't catch mice, the poor duckling became homesick for his mother and felt a great longing to be near water.

So he said good-bye and again took to the air, this time flying toward the duck pond where his mother lived. He had not flown long until he saw below him some beautiful white birds swimming on a pond. Longing to get a closer look he flew down and landed a few feet away from them.

"They are so wonderful and I am so ugly," he thought, "they won't want anything to do with me. But I just want to look at them for a while."

Just then, the beautiful white birds noticed him and began to swim toward him. Ashamed of his ugliness, the duckling bowed his head, expecting the birds to mock and make fun of him. As he looked down at the water, he was surprised to see, not the plump, grey, ugly bird he had always seen before, but the form of a beautiful white swan, just like the birds swimming toward him. Soon, the larger swans were surrounding him, stroking him with their beaks and letting him know they were glad to see him.

The duckling now knew that he was a swan and not a duck at all. Finally, he had found his home and friends he could enjoy and trust. He stayed for a few weeks, and then told his friends he had to leave them for a short while. "I need to go and see my mother," he told them, "I want her to know that she was right."

Hindsight Questions
- What did the ducks think of the baby swan?
- How did their judgment of the baby swan influence how they treated him?
- How did this influence how the baby swan thought and felt about himself?

Insight Questions
- Why did the ducks choose to treat the baby swan so harshly?
- What are some other choices the ducks could have made?
- Why was it difficult for the baby swan to feel good about himself?
- What does the term "appearances can be deceiving" mean?

Foresight Questions
- Why is it a bad idea to worry too much about what others think of you?
- Why is it wrong to judge others by their appearance?

Discussion Opportunity: Judge B. Fore convinced the ducks that the baby swan would amount to nothing. Their opinions, however, were not based on the nature of things. They were thinking he was a duck, but he was not a duck at all, he was a swan. They also falsely assumed that how he looked and moved as a child was how he would always look and move. The wonderful message of this story is that each child is a work in progress. A child who is gangly and awkward will not always be gangly and awkward. A child who is slow at the start may be strong at the finish. And each child's potential is more than he or she can imagine. When adults or other children judge a child on what he or she appears to be at the moment, they do a great disservice to that child and to themselves as well. Character Traits: PR right; RO caring, fairness

ACTIVITY 21

THE NATURE OF THINGS

For the following quizzes, have your students number a piece of paper from 1 through 10. Explain that you are going to read some statements about things many people believe. They are to write a "T" or "F" for each statement, depending on whether they think it is true or false.

21-1 ———————————— Old Wives' Tales ————————————

1. An apple a day will keep the doctor away.
2. Reading in a dim light will hurt your eyes.
3. Eating chocolate will give you zits.
4. Swimming right after eating causes cramps.
5. Brown eggs are more nutritious than white.
6. Touching frogs will give you warts.
7. If you cross your eyes, they may get stuck.
8. Eating too much sugar can cause diabetes.
9. Carrots are good for your eyes.
10. Hot meals are more nourishing than cold.

Answers for Old Wives' Tales

1. F. Apples are a healthy addition to one's diet but provide no special protection against illness
2. F. According to the American Academy of Ophthalmology: "Reading in a dim light cannot any more harm the eyes than taking a photograph in a dim light can hurt the camera."
3. F. Eating sweets does not cause pimples or acne. Zits are caused by glandular disorders and stress.
4. F. Cramps are caused by fatigue, cold, overexertion, being out of shape, or by overeating. If you happen to be swimming when cramps occur from one of these causes, it could be dangerous.
5. F. The color of the shell has nothing to do with the nutrition of the egg.
6. F. Bumps on frogs look like warts, but warts are caused by viruses easily passed among children.
7. F. Individuals who have the muscular control to cross their eyes are least likely to have crossed eyes.
8. F. Managing sugar intake is a problem for diabetics, but eating sugar does not cause diabetes. Diabetes is caused by the body not manufacturing adequate insulin to control how the body metabolizes sugar.
9. T. Carrots contain a large amount of vitamin A. Vitamin A is essential for healthy epithelial tissue in the cornea and conjunctiva of the eyes.
10. F. Hot or cold, foods usually offer the same nourishment, unless, perhaps, the food is overcooked.

Reference Books for *The Nature of Things*

Cross Your Fingers, Spit in Your Hat by Alvin Schwartz, published by J.B. Lippincott
Don't Sing Before Breakfast, Don't Sleep in the Moonlight by Lila Perl, published by Clarion Books
'Old Wives' Tales, the Truth Behind Common Notions by Sue Castle, published by Citadel Press
The Simon and Schuster Book of Facts and Fallacies by Roda and Leda Blumberg, published by Simon and Schuster
The Unhuggables, the Truth about Snakes, Slugs, Spiders, and Other Animals that are Hard to Love published by the National Wildlife Foundation.

21-2 — Fact or Fancy in Animal Lore

1.   Whales spout water.
2.   Dinosaurs are the largest animals to ever live.
3.   Penguins live at the north pole.
4.   Camels store water in their humps.
5.   Opposums use their their tails to hang from tree limbs
6.   Goats eat tin cans.
7.   Bulls attack when they see red.
8.   Horses sleep standing up.
9.   The lion is king of the jungle.
10.   Elephants drink water through their trunks.

Answers for Fact or Fancy in Animal Lore

1. F.   When whales come up to breathe, they blow out air, which sprays any water that may be above them.
2. F.   The largest whale is 150 tons and 100 feet long. The largest dinosaur was only 75 tons, and 70 feet long.
3. F.   Wrong direction. Penguins live in South Africa, South America, Australia, New Zealand, and the South Pole.
4. F.   The camel's hump consists of fat, which the camel digests to obtain the liquid contained therein.
5. F.   The oppossum's tail is not strong enough to hang from. It is for support and balance when climbing trees.
6. F.   Goats like glue and nibble at tin cans to eat the glue on them, but they cannot eat tin cans.
7. F.   Bulls are color blind. They do not attack because the cape is red, but because they are irritated by the noise of the crowd, the waving of the cape, and being poked with sharp spears.
8. F.   Horses may doze while standing, but must lie down to sleep. Most lie down and get up several times a night.
9. F.   Lions never live in jungles. They live on open bush areas and grassy plains.
10. F.   An elephant sucks water into its trunk and then sprays the water into its mouth.

Hindsight Questions
- How many got all the answers correct?
- Were there any questions everyone missed?

Insight Questions
- How do incorrect opinions get to be commonly believed?
- How important is correct information in forming a correct opinion?

Foresight Questions
- Why is it important to question what we believe from time to time?
- What are some ways we can check on the accuracy of our opinions?

> **Discussion Opportunity:** Nature, not opinion, determines whether something is true or false. Even the reference books and the answers provided above do not present the whole truth. It is so easy, when we get a little information, or have someone we believe tell us something, to think we know all we need to know on a given subject. This is what Judge B. Fore tries to get us to think. If he can get us to form opinions based on false or insufficient information, he can lead us to make bad choices. Character Traits: PR duty; T dependability

ACTIVITY 22

THE FIRST BALLOON ASCENT

In the early morning hours of August 23, 1783, Benjamin Franklin gathered with some five thousand others near Paris, France, to watch the first public demonstration of raising a hot-air balloon. Franklin wrote to a friend describing his experience:

"At five o'clock notice was given to the spectators, by the firing of two cannon, that the cord was about to be cut. And presently the [balloon] was seen to rise. A little rain had wet it, so that it shone, and made an agreeable appearance. It diminished in size as it rose, till it entered the clouds, when it seemed to me scarce bigger than an orange, and soon after became invisible, the clouds concealing it.

"The multitude separated, all well satisfied and delighted with the success of the experiment. . . .

"P.S. . . . It is said the country people who saw [the balloon] fall were frightened, [they] thought from its bounding a little when it touched the ground that there was some living animal in it, and attacked it with stones and knives, so that it was much mangled."

Bigelow, John, *The Works of Benjamin Franklin*, New York: G.P. Putnams Sons, 1904, V.10, P. 157,158.

Hindsight Questions
* What opinion did the country people have of the balloon when it landed?
* What did they do as a result of this opinion?

Insight Questions
* Why is the unknown sometimes frightening?
* How do mistaken opinions sometimes lead us to do foolish things?

Foresight Questions
* What might the country people have done differently?

> **Discussion Opportunity:** Fear of the unknown can lead people to refuse to do things they might otherwise enjoy or benefit from. It can also lead people to do things that are harmful to themselves and others. It takes a certain courage to inquire and seek more information before making choices in these situations. Judge B. Fore will try to get you to make a choice before you get the information you need to make an informed choice. Character Traits: PR duty

CHOOSING TO DEVELOP
THE SEVEN C SKILLS
FOR THINKING CLEARLY

Section Two

LEARNING OBJECTIVES FOR SECTION TWO

Understand what the Seven C Skills are and their importance

Possess a knowledge of how to develop the Seven C Skills

Possess a desire to develop the Seven C Skills

SECTION OVERVIEW

In *The Descent of Man,* Charles Darwin wrote, "The highest possible stage in moral culture is when we recognize that we ought to control our thoughts. . . .Whatever makes any bad action familiar to the mind, renders its performance so much the easier." Unfortunately, thoughts that uplift, inspire, motivate, and encourage us to be better human beings seem to require greater effort than do contrary thoughts. To guide our thoughts to higher ground requires a strength of mind that is something more than I.Q. In his book by the same name, Daniel Goleman refers to this strength of mind as "emotional intelligence." Emotional intelligence is the ability to manage or control our thoughts and feelings and guide them to positive outcomes. To acquire this kind of mental and emotional strength requires a sustained and disciplined effort. It is not an accident of birth. Conscious choices must be made. One of these choices is the decision to develop seven specific thinking skills—Criticism, Concentration, Curiosity, Creativity, Communication, Control, and Correction.

Criticism:	The ability to consider, study, question, compare, and form accurate judgments as to the value or worth of things
Concentration:	The ability to pay close attention and stay on task
Curiosity:	The ability to wonder, inquire, explore, and seek out new information
Creativity:	The ability to imagine, originate, invent, and design new things
Communication:	The ability to share ideas and knowledge through listening, speaking, reading, and writing
Control:	The ability to govern one's own thoughts and feelings
Correction:	The ability to make necessary changes in one's beliefs, choices, and actions to improve the results

The Seven C Skills are largely available to anyone who wishes to acquire them. *Desire and effort are far more important than intellectual capacity.* Therefore, it is necessary to help young people: 1) Understand the importance of acquiring these seven skills, 2) Know how to develop them, and 3) Commit to a life-long process of skill development that will greatly challenge them, but will also take them to otherwise unachievable heights of accomplishment and personal satisfaction.

ACTIVITY 23

INTRODUCING THE SEVEN C SKILLS

23-1 _____ Introducing the CT Team _____

ADVANCE PREPARATION: *Photocopy page 43 and cut out the scripts for each character. Prepare an overhead of page 46 for readers to reference while reading each part. Select a student to read each part.*

Set the stage by describing Big D and the Seven C's as an emergency team of specialists whose job it is to save people from the Stink'n Think'n Gang. After the parts are read, either in small groups or as a class, develop a list of activities that would help them learn the Seven C skills. Use this list in conjunction with the activities in this section. As you become more familiar with the Seven C Skills, you will find frequent opportunity to refer to them in the course of regular class activity.

Hindsight Questions
* What are the Seven C Skills of Thinking Clearly?

Insight Questions
* How important is desire in learning the C skills?
* Why is each skill important to you?

Foresight Questions
* How can controlling your thinking help you make better choices?
* How can curiosity help you learn more in school?

Discussion Opportunity: Explain to your students that the most important thing they do every day is make choices. The quality of their choices is directly influenced by the quality of their thinking skills. Faulty thinking generally leads to poor choices with unhappy consequences. To do better requires the ability to think clearly and to understand things as they really are rather than how we may imagine them. You may wish to discuss Franklin's quote on page 3. Character Traits: PR duty; SR self-reliance

---

23-2 _____ Put on Your Thinking Cap _____

ADVANCE PREPARATION: *Gather together pieces of cardboard (cereal boxes and poster board work well), glue, and scissors. Photocopy page 45 for each student. Have them color, cut out and paste each character on a thin piece of cardboard. Ask each child to bring in a hat to use as their thinking cap. As you work on each skill, have them pin the appropriate medallion on their hat. Begin each activity by saying, "Put on your thinking cap for creativity (etc.). We are going to practice our creative skills today by . . . ." Alternatively, you may wish to make necklaces of the medallions by running a piece of yarn through a hole in the top.*

Introducing the CT Team

Desire
Thank you for inviting us here today. My name is Captain Desire. Team members just call me "Big D." I'm captain of the Clear Thinking Team. Our job is to protect you against the Stink'n Think'n Gang. I motivate team members to keep alert and be on the job at all times. No vacation time for us. Each member of the CT Team has a specific job to do and every member of the team must work together closely if we are to give you the protection you need. Let's have each member of the CT team tell you what they do.

Control
Good (morning/afternoon). I'm Control. I have three jobs. First, I help you keep your emotions in check. For example, if someone gets angry and doesn't call on me, the Stink'n Think'n Gang can take control. When this happens, people sometimes say and do hurtful things. Second, I help you keep your mind occupied with worthwhile thoughts so it doesn't just wander aimlessly around. Third, I tell the other members of the team when to get involved and what they need to do.

Concentration
Hi! I'm Concentration. Anytime someone wants to learn or do something that requires skill or effort I am sure to be there. Almost nothing of any real importance is ever done without some help from me. It's a good job. I like it, though I am constantly amazed at how seldom people really use me.

Communication
My name is Communication. Listening, speaking, reading, and writing—these are the tools of my trade. The better people are in using these tools, the more I can help them. Of the four, I believe listening is the most important. But all are necessary for making good choices.

Curiosity
Curiosity's my name! Inquiry's my game! My job is to find out how things work, and why things are the way they are. I ask lots of questions. For example, I want to know who did what and why. Then I want to know how they did it, and where and when. It's a fun job and takes me lots of interesting places.

Creativity
Hey! Creativity here! When the person needs a new tool or machine, it's up to me to invent it. When there is a problem to solve, it's up to me to figure out how. I also help people write beautiful music and great literature, and paint pictures and design buildings. You can see I am kept pretty busy.

Criticism
Just call me Crit. My specialty is discovering truth and detecting error. To do this I carefully study things people tell me. I question, compare, and consider what makes most sense and which is best. I then help you form judgments so you can make good choices.

Correction
Hi! I'm Correction. Whenever the Stink'n Think'n Gang throws you off course, it's my job to help you get back on track. One of the hardest things for many people is to say, "I was wrong" or "I'm sorry." Since everyone makes mistakes, I'm kept very, very busy. Or at least, I should be. Some people do not keep me as busy as they need to.

The CT Team at Work

Present the following situations to your students. Ask them to identify which members of the Stink'n Think'n Gang are working on each individual. Then discuss how the respective members of the CT team might help each individual. You may wish to use this format as a model to consider additional situations more directly relevant to student's interests and needs or to classroom experiences.

Situation 1

Rosita and Miguel were the two final contestants in a spelling contest. Miguel won the contest and then teased Rosita for missing the final word. Rosita exploded in anger, "Miguel, you're a toad." Which member/s of the Stink'n Think'n Gang are working on Miguel and Rosita? How can the CT Team help?

What would curiosity ask?	*(Miguel) How will what I say make Rosita feel?*
	(Rosita) Really now, just how is Miguel like a toad?
What can Communication do?	*(Rosita) Recognize that the word "toad" does not express a true idea of what Miguel is or how what he said made Rosita feel. Find words to express Rosita's real feelings.*
What would Creativity do?	*(Rosita) Find other ways to make self feel good than calling Miguel names or trying to get even with him.*
How can Control help?	*(Miguel) Don't give into temptation to tease*
	(Rosita) Keep emotions in check. Don't give into anger.

Situation 2

An older boy had persuaded Inga to meet him in a vacant lot after school. He said he had something that would really make her feel good if she promised not to tell anyone. Inga is walking to the vacant lot. Which member/s of the Stink'n Think'n Gang are working on Inga? What do you think they have led her to believe? How can the CT Team help Inga?

What would Curiosity ask?	*What did the boy really want? What risk is Inga taking?*
What would Criticism ask?	*Why would Inga trust this boy? Why is she really going? What real benefit does she hope to gain?*
What would Creativity do?	*Imagine various possible outcomes if Inga goes to the vacant lot Explore other options.*
What would Concentration do?	*Listen carefully and pay attention to your conscience.*
What would Communication do?	*Talk to a respected adult or friend about the situation.*
What would Correction do?	*Change directions; think this through before going.*

> **Discussion Opportunity:** The Stink'n Think'n Gang is ever present and if not resisted can lead us to make bad choices. The Seven C Skills, if we possess them, can help us recognize faulty thinking and generate better options for our choices. In situation 1, Miguel builds himself up by pulling Rosita down. In situation 2, Inga needs to recognize the boy is thinking of himself, not her. He will take advantage of her, and may even hurt her if she meets him. Character Traits: PR duty; SR self-denial; RO caring; T honesty

I'm a member of the CT Team
I'm learning to Control my thoughts

I'm a member of the CT Team
I'm learning to Communicate

I'm a member of the CT Team
I'm learning to Concentrate

I'm a member of the CT Team
I'm learning to be Creative

I'm a member of the CT Team
I'm learning to be Curious

I'm a member of the CT Team
I'm learning the skill of Correction

I'm a member of the CT Team
I'm learning the skill of Criticism

CONTROL

CORRECTION

CURIOSITY

CONCENTRATION

COMMUNICATION

CRITICISM

CREATIVITY

ACTIVITY 24

FIVE THINGS I CAN DO

Chalk Talk

Introduce the following discussion with a word association activity. Ask your students to write down the first words that come to their minds when you read the following words: Observe, Study, Question, Compare, and Judge. Afterward explain that these words represent five things they can do to develop the C skill of Criticism. To define it in words children can understand, write the following definition of criticism on the board and discuss each of the five things they can do. In the discussion, ask your students to provide examples from their personal experience of how people can learn to do each of these things.

Criticism: The ability to observe, study, question, compare, and
form judgments as to the value or worth of things

observe	Learn to notice things around me
study	Learn to apply my mind to gaining knowledge
question	Learn to ask questions that increase my understanding
compare	Learn to recognize how things are alike and how they are different
judge	Learn to form opinions of things based on their true merit or worth

Hindsight Questions
* What five skills are required for critical thinking?

Insight Questions
* How can a person begin learning these skills?
* Why are these skills important in avoiding faulty thinking?

Foresight Questions
* Why is it worth the effort to learn these skills?

Discussion Opportunity: Five things children can do to develop the skill of Criticism while they are still young are observe, study, question, compare, and form judgments consistent with the nature of things. One of the great problems many people have is the tendency to form judgments without having made the effort to observe, study, question, and compare. In doing so, they frequently form opinions that are not in accordance with the nature of things. We saw some of the problems that result from this tendency in the first section on faulty thinking. As we learned from Franklin, since right action is dependent on right opinion, one of the most important things we can do in life is to take care that our opinions are in accordance with the nature of things. Character Traits: PR duty; SR self-reliance

ACTIVITY 25

THINK ALONG WITH ZACHARY BLACK

ADVANCE PREPARATION: *Photocopy the story "Think Along with Zachary Black" on page 49.*

1. *Have your students read the poem and write on each of the lines in the left margin which of the five criticism skills (noted at the bottom) Zach is using at that point.*

2. *In addition, you may wish to have them note in the right margin those sections in which Zach is using the following C skills: Curiosity, Communication, Concentration and Correction.*

3. *After the above activities, lead the class in a discussion of which of the Seven C Skills they used in performing the activity.*

Hindsight Questions
• What happened when Zach asked questions of different people?
• What were some things Zach did to keep his thinking on track?

Insight Questions
• Why did Zach feel a need to do these things?
• What does the phrase "whatever we think we are likely to do" mean?

Foresight Questions
• Why is that phrase important to you?
• What are some things you can do to help keep your thinking on track.

Discussion Opportunity: The great importance of developing our thinking skills lies in the statement, "whatever we think we are likely to do." Faulty thinking leads to faulty opinions, which in turn lead to faulty choices. To avoid faulty thinking, it is necessary to develop the Seven C Skills of which Criticism is an important part. Criticism is an important front line defense against the Stink'n Think'n Gang. If we do our homework before forming an opinion, Judge B. Fore has less power over us. Biggs Bigger and Eency Wency Tiny Too have greater difficulty in getting us to blow things out of proportion and Iwannit Now has little opportunity to make us want things that aren't good for us. Similarly, Li Fib and Nameit Blameit cannot get to us so easily. Character Trait: PR duty; SR self-reliance

---

THINK ALONG WITH ZACHARY BLACK

by George L. Rogers
Illustration by Stefanie Eskander

Zach was a curious lad who wanted to know why,
So he asked lots of questions, like "Why do birds fly?"
"Why does one plus one always add up to two?"
And, "Why do zebras and hyenas live in the zoo?"

"Why do people sometimes argue and fight?"
And, "Why are some things wrong and other things right?"
It wasn't always easy for Zach to find out
Why things are and what life's all about.

For, when he asked a parent or teacher, a friend or his brother,
Some said one thing and some said another.
So, Zach carefully observed to see how people lived,
Were they happy or sad from the things that they did?

He learned thoughts and behaviors are so closely connected,
That whatever happens to one, the other is affected.
For one thing is sure and most certainly true,
Whatever we think, we are most likely to do.

So, he felt a great need to keep his thinking on track,
And since he was a smart boy, this Zachary Black,
There are some things he decided to do,
When figuring things out and thinking them through.

Before making up his mind or taking a stand,
Zach studied all sides of the question at hand.
He looked at each matter from every angle he could,
So the decisions he made would more likely be good.

Another thing Zach did that was remarkably sound
He was open to truth, no matter where found.
And whenever he found his thinking was wrong,
He simply changed what he thought and kept moving along.

In this poem are examples of five things that helped Zach develop the C skill of Criticism.
Below is a definition of criticism with those five things underlined. Write the thing he did
in the margin by the sentence or phrase where you think he did it.

Criticism: The ability to <u>observe</u>, <u>study</u>, <u>question</u>, <u>compare</u>, and <u>form judgments</u> as to value or
worth.

ACTIVITY 26

LOOK HIGHER, LOOK FURTHER, LOOK DEEPER

If possible, take your class outside. Allow students 5 to 10 minutes to take notes on what they see by looking up, looking in the distance, and looking closely at what they see on the ground or floor. Ask them to include as much detail in their notes as they can, but only include things they can actually see.

Bring your class inside and write three columns headings—higher, further, and deeper— on the board. List under each everything they saw and note how many saw each thing. Discuss the things most people saw and things only some people saw. Discuss the HIF questions below.

ACTIVITY 27

LOOK SEE, TOUCH FEEL, LISTEN HEAR

27-1.   *Have your students look at an object in the room and ask them to tell you what they see in some detail. For example if the object is a book, how big is it? What color is the cover? What is the book about? Repeat this exercise for several different objects. Discuss the HIF questions below.*

27-2.   ADVANCE PREPARATION: *Place three or four familiar items in a sock and put a rubber band around the top of the sock. In class, pass the sock around and have students note on a piece of paper the things they can identify in the sock. After everyone has had an opportunity to feel the sock, note on the board which items they identified. Discuss the HIF questions below.*

27-3.   *Have your students be very quiet and listen to what they can hear. After a couple of minutes, have them tell you what they heard. See how many different sounds they were able to identify. Discuss the HIF questions below.*

Hindsight Questions
- What did you have to do to observe or notice things?

Insight Questions
- Why did different people observe or notice different things?

Foresight Questions
- How can the ability to observe, study, question, and compare help you in forming opinions?

Discussion Opportunity: The ability to make good choices is dependent on our ability to forsee the consequences of our choices. By noticing what other people do and what happens as a result of their choices, it is often possible to learn from their experience. To do this requires the C skill of Criticism; that is, the ability to observe, study, question, compare, and form judgments about the nature of things. The better our observation, study, questioning, and comparison skills, the better our judgments, and in turn, the better our choices will be. Character Traits: PR duty; SR self-reliance

ACTIVITY 28

PRO & CON

In making choices, a useful technique is to compare reasons in favor of the choice (Pro) with reasons against the choice (Con) by writing them on a piece of paper next to each other. Illustrate with the example below, have students practice with personal choices, and then discuss the HIF questions.

Should I stick up for Marcie when other kids call her names?

PRO	CON
1. I feel sorry for Marcie.	1. The other kids may not like me.
2. I feel what they are doing is wrong.	2. They may turn against me.
3. I would be ashamed if I didn't.	
4. It will help Marcie feel better.	

ACTIVITY 29

TAKE A TEST RUN

One way to test opinions or choices before acting on them is to select three people whose judgment you respect, but may not necessarily agree with. Explain to each what you are thinking and ask for their opinion. If they disagree, try to understand why. Remember, you are not looking for support for your idea, you are trying to find out what problems you may encounter if you act on it. Discuss the HIF Questions.

Hindsight Questions
- What did you learn from this activity?

Insight Questions
- When might doing a pro and con comparison or taking a test run be helpful?

Foresight Questions
- How can doing a pro con comparison or taking a test run help you make better choices?

Discussion Opportunity: Iwannit Now and Judge B. Fore encourage us to form opinions and make choices before we really understand the consequences of what we are choosing. Comparing the pros and cons and talking to others who may help us see things in a different light can help us overcome their influence and make better choices. Critical thinking skills that include observation, study, questioning, comparing, and forming judgments are all involved in this process. Character Traits: PR duty; SR self-reliance

ACTIVITY 30

NO UNINTERESTING THINGS

The woman timidly approached the distinguished looking man. Dressed plainly, almost shabbily, she seemed out of place in the crowd that milled about the man. He was the famed Dr. Louis Agassiz, an internationally famous naturalist. He had just completed a lecture to an audience of well-dressed, well-educated people among whom the woman felt like an onion in a petunia patch.

Waiting until Dr. Agassiz was finally alone, the woman approached him, not knowing quite what to say. But deep inside her was a yearning to do something more with her life and his words had brought those yearnings to the surface. It was this desire that gave her the courage to walk up to him, for by nature she was timid and quiet. As she drew closer, he turned to look at her and smiled, "Yes, madam, how may I help you?"

"I...I...liked your talk Dr. Agassiz. It. . .it was really interesting," she stammered, "I never had a chance in life to learn very much about things like that."

"Thank you, I'm glad you found it interesting," he replied and then in a kindly voice he began to question her a little about her life. He discovered that for the last fifteen years she had helped her sister run a boarding house and that most of her time had been spent peeling potatoes and chopping onions on the bottom step of the kitchen stairs. "Where do your feet rest when performing these duties?" he asked.

"On the glazed brick," she answered.

"What is glazed brick?

"I don't know."

With this answer, Dr. Agassiz handed her his card and asked her to write him a letter concerning the nature of glazed brick.

The woman took the good doctor seriously and began an adventure that took her from libraries to museums to brickyards. After a few weeks, she mailed Dr. Agassiz a 36-page paper on the subject of glazed brick. Dr. Agassiz thought it was the best he had ever seen and had the paper published. He then sent the woman a check for $250 with a note that read, "What is under those bricks?"

"Ants," she wrote back.

"Tell me about the ants," he replied in a return note.

So began an intensive study of ants. She discovered there are nearly 2500 different kinds of ants, some so small, you could place three together on a pin and others, an inch long that march in armies a half mile wide. Some ants are blind. Some ants get wings on the afternoon that they die. She even discovered peasant ants that serve aristocrat ants that live in the neighborhood. The more she studied, the more she became intrigued with what she was learning. By and by, she had written a 360-page book on ants. Her work proved so interesting, it was published and provided her sufficient royalties to enable her to travel and do many of the things she had always wanted to do.

This little story beautifully illustrates the important truth, "There are no uninteresting things, only uninterested people."

Hindsight Questions
- When did the woman first pay close attention to glazed brick and ants? Why?

Insight Questions
- What does the statement "There are no uninteresting things, only uninterested people" mean?

Foresight Questions
- How can developing an active curiosity help you have a richer, more interesting life?

Discussion Opportunity: The thing that changed in this story was the person, not the glazed bricks or the ants. They stayed the same as they always were. The woman was not naturally interested in either but, when faced with a reason to learn about them, she developed an interest. Iwannit Now will try to limit our attention to those things that naturally interest us. At the same time, Eency Wency Tiny Too will try to tell us that anything that doesn't naturally interest us isn't important. To fight their influence we need to call upon the Seven C Skills to help us. The ability to Concentrate is greatly increased by Curiosity coupled with the ability to observe things. When Dr. Agassiz aroused her curiosity, the woman developed the powers of concentration. Character Traits: PR ownership; Sr self-reliance

ACTIVITY 31

TWO KINDS OF INTEREST

Motivation and concentration, while not synonymous, are both greatly dependent on interest. In the normal course of daily activities, there are abundant opportunities for students to utilize the skill of concentration. Failure to do so is usually a result of the lack of interest or motivation. There are two kinds of interest that will generally motivate a person to pay close attention to a task, whether the task is learning or doing. One is natural interest, the other is interest derived from a felt need to know.

31-1 .... Natural Interest ....

When a person is doing something he or she naturally enjoys, it is easy to pay attention. So, one way to make a task more interesting is to find something in that task that appeals to your natural interests. After the following activities explore ways each talent my be used in ordinary daily tasks.

1. *Set aside time in class and have each student present a talent or hobby. After each presentation, allow class members to ask the presenter questions about how he or she got interested in this activity and what he or she has had to do to develop some skill or knowledge about it.*

2. *Assign students to write a one page paper about something they have done or seen that really interested them. In the paper, have them tell what it was that interested them and why.*

Hindsight Questions
- To what extent was personal interest a common factor in what each person likes or is learning to do?

Insight Questions
- Why is it easier to pay attention to something you are interested in?
- Why are different people interested in different things?

Foresight Questions
- When may it be important to pay attention to things you have less interest in?
- How can you learn to pay attention to things you have less interest in?

31-2 _____ Need to Know _____

Most teachers assume the responsibility of trying to find different ways to make a subject of interest to their students. However, assuming full responsibility can be a difficult burden. The following activities will help students recognize why it may be to their advantage to learn things they are being taught.

1. *In introducing a new topic, assign students to find out how and when this information may be needed or how it may be helpful to them, either now or in the future. Have them talk to parents, teachers, librarians, and other adults. Discuss their findings.*

2. *Tell the class why you think this knowledge is important. Break the class into small groups with the assignment to prepare a class presentation to illustrate the advantages of possessing and the disadvantages of not possessing this particular set of knowledge.*

3. *Invite guest speakers (experts) to talk about the importance of the topic and their need to know.*

4. *After teaching a lesson, use HIF questions to help your students focus on what they have just learned, why you have tried to teach it to them, and how it might help them in the future. Following are some generic HIF questions you may draw on.*

Hindsight Questions
• What did we just do? • What did we just learn? • What did we just talk about?

Insight Questions
• Why do you need to know this? • Why did we spend time learning this?
• Why am I required to teach you this? • How can you use this information?

Foresight Questions
• How can knowing this make a difference to you in the future?
• Why might not knowing this be a disadvantage to you in the future?

Discussion Opportunity: It is easier to pay attention to things we are interested in than things we are not. Each of us has different interests and sometimes we all need to learn things in which we have little or no natural interest. But, when something is important to know and we fail to learn it, we put ourselves at risk. The key is to find something in the task that interests us. Simply recognizing we have a need to know can increase our interest in learning something. Many times, just asking a few questions can help us develop an interest. Often it is possible to discover interests we didn't even know we had. But, Judge B. Fore will try to convince us we're not interested before we even give it a try. Name It Blame It may even try to convince us that we're not smart enough to learn it. Eency Weency Tiny will tell us it's not important to know. Iwannit Now and Biggs Bigger will try to get us to think others things are more important. To overcome their influence we need to enlist the help of Curiosity, Creativity, Concentration, and Control to get our thinking turned around. This will require us to take ownership of our thoughts and feelings and to exercise a high degree of initiative and self-control. It may even require persistence and patience. But these are the very qualities that make it possible to truly succeed in life. Character Traits: PR duty; SR self-reliance

BIOGRAPHY

WHO AM I?

The following biographical sketches are written in the first person. Read each sketch to your students and have them guess each person's name.

32-1   Madam Curie

I was used to hard work and long hours. As Pierre and I worked side by side, the days and weeks were filled with excitement, even though the work was difficult and demanding. In my earlier work, I had discovered what appeared to be a new element, but was not able to demonstrate it in a manner that could be shown to others. Pierre stopped his own research projects to help me. We had children to care for and our little laboratory was nothing more than an old shed with an earthen floor and flaking plaster walls. The roof leaked when it rained and the only heat came from a rusty old stove.

Nevertheless, each morning I could hardly wait to get to work. For nearly four years, I spent a large part of each day outside in a windy courtyard stirring boiling chemicals in a large pot with a long iron rod. I would then pour the strange-looking matter into large glass jars that Pierre and I would study for hours. Not knowing the cause at the time, we often received burns on our hands, faces, and other parts of our bodies from these fluids. Of course, we now know that these burns were caused by radium, the new element we discovered. Actually, in the end, we discovered not one but two new elements, polonium and radium. Who am I?

Hindsight Questions
- What kind of conditions did Madam Curie have to work under?
- What was her attitude about her work?

Insight Questions
- Why was Madam Curie willing to work in those conditions?
- Why do you think Madam Curie was so excited about what she was doing?
- Why did she have to pay attention to what she was doing?

Foresight Questions
- What would have happened if Madam Curie had decided to give up?
- What is the reward of staying with a task and doing it well?

32-2 — Michaelangelo

I am perhaps best known for my painting of the ceiling of the Sistine Chapel in the Vatican. This is a work I undertook unwillingly. I had not painted for over twenty years and did not consider myself a qualified artist. Furthermore, this project took me away from my first love of sculpturing. Finally, I knew what a huge undertaking it would be. I only undertook this work because Pope Julius gave me no other choice.

On May 10, 1508 I began work on the ceiling. I decided to use the fresco method of painting. It is a method in which I would apply wet plaster to the ceiling and then paint the wet plaster. As the paint and plaster dried together, the painting became an integral part of the ceiling itself. Although this is a very tedious manner of painting, it is also very permanent. At the beginning of the project, I had two assistants helping me paint, but I had to redo much of their work, so I decided to just do the whole project myself. For nearly four and one half years, I worked on a scaffold fifty feet off the ground, standing in a low, bent down position for hours each day, plastering and painting an area of over 5,800 square feet. Who am I?

Hindsight Questions
- Why did Michaelangelo not want to paint the Sistine Chapel?
- What did Michaelangelo have to do to paint the ceiling of the chapel?
- How long did it take him to complete the task?

Insight Questions
- Why did Michaelangelo not chose a less difficult and time-consuming manner in which to paint the ceiling of the Sistine chapel?
- Why did Michaelangelo invest so much effort into a project he did not even want to do?
- What gave him the ability to pay close attention to what he was doing for long hours each day and to stay on task for four and one half years?

Foresight Questions
- What does it usually cost to do something really well?
- Why is doing something really well usually worth the investment?

Discussion Opportunity: Both Madam Curie and Michaelangelo were required to pay close attention to what they were doing and to stay on task for long periods of time. If they had not done one or the other, they would have failed. These skills are required in doing almost anything of importance. In each case, neither was interested in the task as such. In both cases, the task was dirty, hard work that was tiring and caused physical pain. What interested each of them was the result they were seeking to achieve. Madam Curie experienced opposition from many in the scientific community, partly because she was a woman and partly because other scientists doubted she could find another element. The Stink'n Think'n Gang was working hard on those who found fault with her. Michelangelo, decided he would do well anything he tried. He was not willing to have his name associated with something that was shoddy or carelessly done. Painting the ceiling was something he needed to do, therefore he would do it well. Character Traits: PR duty; SR Self-reliance

ACTIVITY 33

EDISON'S SIX QUESTIONS

As a young boy, Thomas Alva Edison was very curious about things. One time he became very curious about goose eggs. He wanted to know *what* goose eggs were, *what* was in them, *where* they came from, *how* they were made, if they were all made the same way, *why* the goose made them that way, and *why* did the mother goose sit on them.

His mother explained to him that inside the eggs were baby geese and the mother goose sat on the eggs to keep them warm so they would hatch and the baby geese could come out. One day, three-year old, Al as he was called, was in the barnyard, watching a mother goose sitting on some eggs. Occasionally, the mother goose would get up, turn the eggs over, and then sit back down. After awhile, Al heard a "Peep-peep! Peep-peep!" and saw a small, down-covered head, peeking through an egg that had cracked open. He now knew, or at least thought he did, not only the who, what, why, how, and where, but also the *when* of hatching eggs.

Excitedly, Al was up early the next morning and went into the hen house. He removed a couple of eggs from the nest, took some straw, placed it on the ground, placed the eggs in the straw, and sat on them. Patiently, he sat on the eggs, occasionally standing up and turning them as he had seen the mother goose do the day before, but no eggs hatched.

When he was older, Thomas Alva Edison became a great inventor. But he was not good at everything. Math was a serious problem for him and, unfortunately, the field of invention required extensive use of mathematics. The way Edison made up for this weakness is illustrated by a situation that occurred one time in court. A lawyer asked Edison to convert degrees Centigrade to degrees Fahrenheit. Edison answered, "I don't compute such things."

"How do you find out then?" asked the lawyer.

"I ask somebody." replied Edison.

To demonstrate, Edison invited one of his assistants to come forward and compute the conversion.

Hindsight Questions
- What were the six questions that helped Thomas Edison become a great inventor?
- When Edison was not good at something, what did he do?

Insight Questions
- Why is curiosity an important quality for an inventor?
- How can curiosity help people in other fields as well?

Foresight Questions
- Why is it important for you to develop the C skill of curiosity?

Discussion Opportunity: Most children are naturally curious. But to keep this quality alive and develop it into a useful skill requires effort and awareness. The six questions curiosity seeks to answer are very important in thinking clearly. Curiosity is a front line thinking skills in combating the Stink'n Think'n Gang. Curiosity generates the questions the other C skills need to answer. If the Stink'n Think'n Gang can get us to be satisfied with what we already know, they have won the battle.
  ~ter Traits: SR self-reliance

BIOGRAPHY

ABU AND THE WRIGHT BROTHERS

Abu

Sometime in the year 1002, a citizen of Turkistan named Abu alDjawhari climbed to the top of a mosque in the city of Nisabur. He announced to the people below that he would amaze the world by performing a feat never before accomplished. He proceeded to strap two large wooden wings to his body and told the people watching him that he was going to fly. He then leaped from the building into the air.

Abu, Abu, the unfortunate Turk.
With wooden wings that didn't work,
Amidst the birds he tried to soar,
Alas, Abu, he is no more

Hindsight Question
* What happened to Abu when he jumped from the building? Why?

Insight Questions
* What did Abu fail to understand?
* Why might Abu not have understood the law of gravity?
* How forgiving is nature when we do things that are contrary to her laws?

Foresight Questions
* What could Abu have done to avoid getting hurt?
* What questions could Abu have asked?

The Wright Brothers

In 1896, another man died while trying to fly. His name was Otto Lilienthal. Otto Lilienthal had conducted several successful gliding experiments, but still did not possess the understanding of aerodynamics necessary to make safe flight possible. Wilbur and Orville Wright had followed Lilienthal's experiments with close interest. His death stimulated their interest in solving the problems that had made previous efforts to fly so dangerous.

They studied every book and pamphlet on flying they could find. They studied different kinds of flying machines and who had tried to fly them. They wanted to know—What kind of flying machine had been used? How did it work? How well did it work? Where was it flown? When was it flown? and What happened? They wanted to know everything they could about flying. In 1899, they constructed a model biplane with a five-foot wing span which they flew as a kite. They found a place in Kitty Hawk, North Carolina, that was ideally suited for glider experimentation. In 1901, they built a wind tunnel in which they tested over 200 different types of wing surfaces.

Finally, on December 17, 1903, Orville Wright made the first successful flight in a self-powered airplane.

Hindsight Questions
- What questions did Orville and Wilbur ask?
- Why did they want to know?

Insight Questions
- In flying airplanes why is it important to make sure your opinion of things is consistent with the nature of things?
- How forgiving is mother nature if we do not understand her laws?
- How can curiosity improve the quality of your choices?

Foresight Questions
- What are the risks of undisciplined curiosity?
- What is the risk of not being curious enough?

Discussion Opportunity: Abu was curious about what it might be like to fly, but perhaps he was not sufficiently curious about what it takes to fly or what might happen if his attempt was unsuccessful. Many young people get into trouble by having the same kind of curiosity that Abu had. They want to try the experiment, but they do not ask enough questions about what happens if the experiment fails. To avoid disaster, before trying any dangerous experiment a person needs to ask lots of questions of people who know the answers. Iwannit Now wants immediate satisfaction, Curiosity wants to know, Who has done this before? What happened to them? Why? How? Where? When? Judge B. Fore wants you to think you already know the answers. Curiosity wants you to ask people with different points of view. To explore, question, and examine. Character Traits: PR duty; SR self-reliance

---

ACTIVITY 35

THE GOLDEN CALF

Read the following story to your students and then ask them, either in small groups or individually, to develop a list of who, what, why, how, where, and when questions Inspector Uno needs to answer to solve this mystery. After they have prepared their list of questions, taking turns, one question at a time, allow them to ask questions from their lists. When they ask a question you have an answer for, give them the answer. If the question has prerequisite noted, then the prerequisite question has to be asked and answered first.

"Golden Calf Stolen" read the headline in the *London Times*, "Scotland Yard Baffled." The story was about a golden calf on loan to the Art Museum that had been stolen. It was on exhibit as part of a collection of Egyptian statues. The golden calf was particularly valuable. There were no clues as to who had taken it or how. It just vanished. One morning, it was not in its place when the museum opened, yet not one guard had seen anything suspicious during the night. The press was critical of Scotland Yard for moving so slowly.

Inspector Numero Uno looked at the story and said to himself, "Things don't add up here. What are we missing?"

With that, Inspector Uno decided to visit the museum again and look around some more. Arriving at the museum, he stood back from the Egyptian exhibit and just looked around. Above the exhibit were colorful plastic models of the various statues in the exhibit that had been attractively hung from the ceiling to promote the exhibit. He was curious why Mrs. Fitzworthy had made it a point to say the hanging decorations were not her idea when he had complimented her on them. A member of her staff had overheard the conversa-

tion and had come to him privately to tell him that the hanging decorations were indeed Mrs. Fitzworthy's idea and that she had personally directed the placement of each plastic model.

Now, as Inspector Uno looked up at the hanging decorations, he noticed something unusual. He saw that all of the plastic models were swinging slightly from the motion of moving air in the room. But the calf replica was not moving at all.

"That's it!" thought Uno. "The trick is to prove it."

Uno saw Mrs. Fitzworthy standing to one side watching him. He made a quick decision and walked over to her.

"Mrs. Fitzworthy," said Inspector Uno, looking her directly in the eye, "you will be glad to know that I now know where the golden calf is and who took it. We will have the case solved very shortly."

Mrs. Fitzworthy paled slightly and said, "Very good Inspector. Please let me know when you do."

"I most certainly will," he said, then turning to leave he added, "Good day, Mrs. Fitzworthy, I'm sure we'll be talking again very soon."

Key Questions and Answers

1. Q. Why was the plastic replica of the golden calf not blowing in the breeze like the others?
   A. It has some sort of heavy weight inside it.

2. Q. What is the weight inside the plastic replica of the golden calf?
   A. The golden calf.

3. Q. Who could have put the golden calf in the plastic replica?
   A. The person who hung the plastic replicas and/or Mrs. Fitzworthy.

4. Q. Who was the person who hung the plastic replicas?
   A. A day worker hired and supervised by Mrs. Fitzworthy.

5. Q. How could the golden calf have been put in the plastic replica?
   A. Inspector Uno climbed up to the catwalk above the replicas. He observed that the model for the golden calf replica was hung by a rope long enough to be lowered to the statue below it.

6. Q. When could the golden calf have been removed from its pedestal?
   A. Guards made their rounds every hour on the hour. Someone who knew their routine could have removed the golden calf in between their rounds. Most likely it was after the last round of the night as it was not noticed as missing until morning.

7. Q. Where could the golden calf be hidden? (The answer to Q 1 is a prerequisite to answering Q7.)
   A. In the plastic replica of the golden calf hanging above where it had been.

8. Q. Why would Mrs. Fitzworthy have stolen the golden calf?
   A. Inspector Uno had Detective Higgens check into Mrs. Fitzworthy's personal situation. Detective Higgens discovered that Mrs. Fitzworthy is a compulsive gambler and has several hundred thousand dollars in gambling debts which she is under great pressure to pay.

9. Q. How can Inspector Uno prove Mrs. Fitzworthy took the golden calf? (Prerequisite Q#s 1–8)
   A. Inspector checked with the staff and security guards and found that no one had seen Mrs. Fitzworthy leave the museum the night before the robbery or come in the next day, though she had definitely been there both days. While the evidence is not conclusive against Mrs. Fitzworthy, it is quite strong. Inspector Uno gets a court order to remove the hanging replica. Indeed, it has the golden calf in it and both the golden calf and the replica are covered with Mrs. Fitzworthy's fingerprints. Upon questioning, she confesses to the crime.

Hindsight Questions
•   What were the best clues in solving this case?

Insight Questions
•   Why is Curiosity an important requirement for solving problems?
•   Why are Who, What, Why, How, Where, When questions so valuable in getting new information?

Foresight Questions
•   How could Curiosity have helped Mrs. Fitzworthy avoid her gambling problem?

Discussion Opportunity: Curiosity was the key to solving this case. Inspector Uno had to keep asking himself, who could have taken the golden calf, where could it be hidden, why would they have taken it, and so forth. Mrs. Fitzworthy fell victim to the Stink'n Think'n Gang. Iwannit Now got her hooked on gambling, and his partners came in and worked her over. Unable to think clearly, she chose to solve her problems in a way that only created larger problems. Character Traits: PR right; SR self-denial; RO citizenship; T honesty

---

BIOGRAPHY

RAISE THE CHILD AS A MUSLIM

The little brown man in the loincloth on the bed was beginning to revive. He was still very weak from a five-day fast, but he was alert and in good spirits. He was in his seventy-ninth year and fasting at this age was considered a dangerous thing for him. But Gandhi was greatly distressed at the violence that had broken out between the Hindus and Muslims in Calcutta. India had finally won independence from Great Britain, largely through Gandhi's leadership. For many years, Gandhi had constantly taught his people the importance of using non-violent means in resisting British rule. Now that they were free, to have his own people turn against each other in violence was almost more than he could bear. He felt fasting was the only thing he could do that might make a difference.

Fortunately, the people greatly loved Gandhi, and when they heard he was on the verge of death because of them, they quit fighting each other and pledged to work together peacefully to solve their problems. This result greatly pleased Gandhi and he had broken his fast. Though still in bed, he was rapidly gaining strength.

Suddenly, the door to his room broke open. In came a man who appeared to be crazed with madness. Those in the room feared for Gandhi as the man quickly crossed the room to Gandhi's bed.

The man fell on his knees beside the bed and began to weep. "I have sinned, Mahatma," he said. "My own wife and child were killed by the Muslims and in my rage, I killed a small Muslim child. What can I do to bring peace to my soul?"

The Mahatma gently placed his hand on the man's head and softly said, "I will tell you how to find peace. Go find a Muslim child, a homeless child without a family and raise the child as your own. Only, you must be sure to raise the child as a Muslim."

Hindsight Questions
*   Why had Gandhi been fasting?
*   Why was the man who came to Gandhi so miserable?

Insight Questions
*   Why was Gandhi's advice a creative solution to the man's misery?
*   How does hate weaken a person's ability to think and act clearly?
*   What was there in Gandhi's suggestion that could bring peace to the man?

Foresight Questions
*   How can creativity help people solve problems?

Discussion Opportunity: The Stink'n Think'n Gang had gained a terrible influence over large portions of the Hindu and Muslim populations in India at that time. Nameit Blameit was on hand. Each thought of the other as enemies. Each blamed the other for their problems. Biggs Bigger exaggerated their differences and Eency Weency Tiny Too minimized their common interests. The idea of a Hindu raising a Muslim child as a Muslim was a new idea. But Gandhi was a creative problem solver. He knew that the only way for the man to rid himself of the terrible guilt and grief he was experiencing was to love another little boy. Loving an orphaned Muslim boy would help the man redeem himself from the terrible act which he had committed. Character Traits: RO caring, citizenship

ACTIVITY 37

SEQUOYAH CREATES AN ALPHABET

Sequoyah was a successful blacksmith. He had a wife and four sons. He was respected in his community and was doing well in his business. Among other things, Sequoyah was a skilled silversmith and a talented painter. But at the age of thirty nine, Sequoyah's mind was occupied with other things. He had discovered "talking leaves."

"So this is how the white men send messages to each other," thought Sequoyah as he looked at the pieces of paper with words written on them. He recognized immediately the advantages this means of communication offered and wondered to himself why the Cherokees had no written language.

"If white men can send messages to each other," thought Sequoyah, "why can't Cherokees do the same? If we had an alphabet like they do then we could write messages to each other too." This idea sank deeply in Sequoyah's mind and he began to work on developing a Cherokee alphabet.

For several years, Sequoyah studied the Cherokee language and identified 86 separate sounds, which used in different combinations formed all the words in the Cherokee language. He then set to work designing characters to represent each of these sounds. Since he had no

paper, he had to carve his figures on the smooth insides of tree bark.

In his work, however, Sequoyah met with considerable opposition from many of his people. Some thought he was crazy, others thought he had fallen under the spell of a witch. One day, in a fit of rage, his wife threw all of his carved symbols into a fire. Sequoyah was forced to leave his village. The gossip, scorn, and anger were too much for him. Finding an old cabin several miles from his village, Sequoyah continued his work, ignoring the teasing and taunts until one night several villagers burned his cabin. Again, all of his work was destroyed.

Sequoyah moved to Arkansas and continued his work on developing symbols for the Cherokee alphabet. Sequoyah was over fifty now. It took him twelve years to complete the alphabet, but it proved to be so sensible, students could learn it in just a few days. The Old and New Testament, along with many important documents, were translated into the Cherokee language. Sequoyah taught his alphabet to hundreds of his fellow Cherokees and eventually saw large numbers of his people become able to read and write in their own language.

Hindsight Questions
• Why did Sequoyah feel it was so important for his people to have a written language?

Insight Questions
• Why did the ability to read and write gave white people an advantage over Sequoyah's people?
• Which of the Seven C Skills did Sequoyah have to use to create a new language?

Foresight Questions
• How can the ability to read and write be an advantage to you in life?
• Why is it important to develop your creative abilities?

Discussion Opportunity: Sequoyah realized that the ability to read and write gives people power by making it easier to acquire new knowledge and to share ideas with others. Developing a new alphabet required him to use all of the Seven C Skills, but creativity, the ability to imagine, originate, and develop new things was especially important. Character Traits: SR self-reliance RO citizenship

ACTIVITY 38

LOUIS BRAILLE'S GREAT ACHIEVEMENT

Louis was pleased. He knew he finally had it. It had taken him several long years of hard work, but now it was finished. Louis stood up and stretched his body. It was almost dawn and he was tired. As so often in the past, he had worked most of the night. As Louis stood there, he thought back many years, to when he was just a child.

He thought back to his first day of school. He was anxious, frightened, but also excited. In Paris in 1819 there were not many opportunities for blind children to go to school. Although he was only ten years old and it was hard to leave his parents to live full time at the school, Louis remembered how fortunate he felt. Now he could go to school like other children.

Next, Louis thought back to when he had lost his eyesight. He had been only three years old. He had been playing in his father's leather shop when he picked up a sharp tool and accidentally poked himself in the eye. Infection and nerve damage robbed him of sight in both eyes and he was totally blind. Louis had been blind so long, he couldn't remember what it was like to see. But he remembered how cheated he felt in not being able to read.

Louis had a hungry mind and wanted to learn new things. He remembered how excited he was when he first began to read by feeling large raised letters. As Louis ran his fingers over the letters, he began to learn the alphabet and then, little by little, new words. Louis also remembered how unhappy he was when he began to realize how slow this method of reading really was. Even so, it was better than not being able to read at all. There was so much Louis wanted to know, so much he wanted to learn, and reading was one of the best ways for a person to learn.

As Louis thought back, he remembered the day that Charles Barbier, a young French artillery officer had come to the school. Barbier had come to demonstrate a system of raised dots he had developed for sending military messages. It was useful for being able to read messages in the dark and it was thought it might be of some help to the blind. Louis had been very excited and spent a lot of time learning the system. But he soon found the system was too limited to be of any real benefit. He knew the idea was a good one, but it would need many changes before it would work.

It was then that Louis decided that, if he made the effort, he could find some way of improving Barbier's system of raised dots. So he set to work. His goal was to create letters and words with raised dots that blind people could use to read. In a way it was like trying to create a whole new alphabet.

By this time Louis had become a part-time teacher in the school he had been attending and was also the organist in his church. Louis reflected on how he had used every spare hour, often working until late in the night on his project. It had taken him several years, but now he had it. He knew it would work. His system consisted of various combinations of six dots arranged in different ways for each letter of the alphabet. The letter A consisted of one dot. The letter B was two dots, one over the other. C was two dots side by side. Each dot was created by piercing a sharp tool into a heavy piece of paper. When the paper was turned over, the raised dots formed the respective letter.

"I can now use this system to teach other children who can't see how to read," thought the twenty-year-old Louis Braille, little realizing how much benefit people all over the world would eventually derive from his work.

Hindsight Questions
- How did not being able to read make Louis Braille feel?
- What did Louis Braille actually end up creating?

Insight Questions
- Why is the ability to read so important?
- Why did Braille spend so much time and effort to create a new alphabet for the blind?
- Which of the Seven C Skills did Louis Braille need to create the Braille system?

Foresight Questions
- How can developing the skill of creative problem solving help you in your life?

> **Discussion Opportunity:** Creative problem solving is the basis for most human progress, whether individually or as a whole. Louis Braille had a hunger for knowledge. He was still a teenager when he decided to find a better way for people with sight problems to read and write. He picked up on an idea he had learned about and, with a great deal of effort and time, developed it into a new alphabet for the blind. Since then, literally millions of people have benefitted from this form of communication. Character Traits: SR self-reliance; RO citizenship

ACTIVITY 39

IS THAT WHAT I SAID?

Seat students in a circle. Explain that you will whisper a message into the ear of one student. That student will whisper the same message into the ear of the student on his or her right, and so on around around the circle back to the student who started the message. Have the last student repeat the message to the whole class and then have the first person tell them the original message. The rule is that the message will be whispered only once to each student, so it is necessary for the person giving the message to whisper it clearly and for the person receiving it to listen carefully.

Hindsight Questions
- How different was the ending message from the beginning message?

Insight Questions
- Why was there a difference between the two?
- How reliable is second-hand and third-hand information for making important choices?

Foresight Questions
- Why is it important to develop your listening skills?

> **Discussion Opportunity:** Listening skills are extremely important in communicating with others. If we misunderstand what others are saying, it is easy for the Stink'n Think'n Gang to mislead us into believing things that aren't true. Whenever possible, it is helpful to get information from the original source and to make sure we really understand what is being said. Character Traits: RO duty; T dependability

ACTIVITY 40

WHILE AS A CHILD

40-1 _____ Lincoln Tried to Understand _____

"Among my earliest memories, I remember how when a mere child, I used to get irritated when anybody talked to me in a way that I could not understand. I can remember going to my little bedroom, after hearing the neighbors talk of an evening with my father. I would spend a large part of the night trying to make out the exact meaning of what they had said.

"I could not sleep, when I got on such a hunt for an idea, until I had caught it. When I thought I had got it, I was not satisfied until I had repeated it over and over again. I had to put it in language plain enough, as I thought, for any boy I knew to understand."

This was of some use to Lincoln when, as President of the United States, he was able to explain difficult ideas in simple language that almost anyone could understand.

Hindsight Questions
•   What did Abraham Lincoln do as a child to make sure he understood what people were saying?

Insight Questions
•   Why would Lincoln put so much effort into understanding an idea?
•   Which of the Seven C Skills did Lincoln use in this exercise?

Foresight Questions
•   How can this kind of effort help a person make better choices?

40-2 _____ Benjamin Loved to Read _____

"From a child, I was fond of reading, and all the money that ever came into my hands was ever laid out in books. Pleased with the *Pilgrim's Progress,* my first collection was of John Bunyan's works in separate little volumes. . . . .Plutarch's lives. . . . I read abundantly and I still think that time spent to great advantage. There also was a book of DeFore's, called an *Essay on Projects,* and another of Dr. Mather's, called *Essay's To Do Good,* which perhaps gave me a turn of thinking that had an influence on some of the principle events of my life."

Hindsight Questions
•   Which book had an important influence on Benjamin Franklin's life?

Insight Questions
•   Why do you think Franklin was fond of reading?
•   What do you think he gained from the books he read?

Foresight Questions
•   How can reading influence your life?

BIOGRAPHY

DADDY, MY NOSE ITCHES!

The man running through the hall in his undershorts was shouting, "Daddy, my nose itches. She said, 'Daddy, my nose itches.'" Within seconds, doctors and nurses were running toward the man and followed him into a nearby hospital room.

In the room was the cot in which he had been sleeping, and a hospital bed in which his four-year-old daughter, Beth Usher, was lying. As her father came back in the room repeating again and again, "She said, 'Daddy my nose itches.'" she looked up at him, smiled weakly and said, "It does itch. A lot!"

The year was 1985. A few months earlier, Beth had fallen from a swing. The bump on her head had been small and hardly noticeable. But, shortly after, Beth began having seizures. Her parents sought medical help, but nothing seemed to make a difference. Beth's seizures became more frequent and more severe. Her parents were worried and didn't know what to do. Beth's mother spent a lot of time at the library trying to understand what was happening and find out if there were any cures that could help Beth. In her research, she read about a surgical procedure called hemospherics that seemed like it might help their daughter. She also learned about a team of pediatric neurosurgeons at Johns Hopkins in Baltimore who were successful in performing hemospheric operations, a delicate and difficult operation on the brain that few surgeons had the skill and courage to undertake.

Interestingly, the chief of pediatric neuro-surgery at Johns Hopkins was a young African-American doctor, Ben Carson. In elementary school, Ben had been a good boy, but he was also at the bottom of his class. It was a painful and difficult experience for him every time he received his grades on a project or test. Then two things happened that changed his life. One, he got glasses, which made it possible for him to see things more clearly. By getting glasses, his grades moved from an F to D in math. Ben was very encouraged, but his mother said it was not good enough.

One evening she turned off the TV and told Ben and his brother they could only watch three television programs a week. When the boys protested, she added that she was going to require them to read at least two books a week. This was not something that either of the boys wanted to do, but it became a major turning point in Ben's life.

For one, he became interested in science books which laid an important foundation for his future career. Secondly, his grades began to improve dramatically and, in time, he was performing at the top of his class. This made it possible for him to be accepted into medical school.

Now Ben was at the top of his profession as a gifted surgeon. Because of his skills in performing this most difficult brain operation, young Beth would not only live, but would have a normal life. Dr. Ben Carson had made this remarkable journey from the bottom of his class to the top of his profession as a pediatric neurosurgeon, all because he had developed a love of learning and a love of reading.

Hindsight Questions
- How did Beth's mother learn about the doctors at Johns Hopkins?
- What did Ben's mother require of him when he was young?

Insight Questions
- How did reading more help improve Ben's grades in school?
- What would have happened if Beth's mother had not known how to read?

Foresight Questions
- Would reading more books and watching less TV help other people besides Ben?

ACTIVITY 42

WHO'S IN CONTROL?

43-1   TV Remote Control

Have a student demonstrate and explain the use of a remote control device for changing TV channels.

43-2   Remote Control Car

Invite a student to bring to class and demonstrate how a remote-controlled car works.

Hindsight Questions
- How was it possible to control the TV/car?

Insight Questions
- Why is it important to be able to control things?
- What is the difference between external and internal control?

Foresight Questions
- Which kind of control will enable you to be most happy?

43-3   Too Many Its

Allow your students to select one of their favorite games to play that requires someone to be "It," such as "Red Light, Green Light," "Do As I'm Doing," "Tag," or "Hide 'N Go Seek." Have them play the game normally for a bit, then have two or more people be "It" at the same time.

Hindsight Questions
- What happened when there was more than one person who was it?

Insight Questions
- Why do games have rules?
- How do rules help people work together more cooperatively?
- Why does there need to be someone who is "It" to enforce rules at school and home?

Foresight Questions
- How can following the rules help you have more fun?
- What can you do when the rules don't seem fair?

Discussion Opportunity: Things require external control. People need internal control. Iwannit Now may try to convince us we should be "It" instead of someone else, or Eency Weency Tiny Too may try to convince us that rules don't matter. Criticism helps us to understand that rules can help us work together, Curiosity can help us discover which rules work best, and Creativity can help us imagine rules that work for everyone. Character Traits: RO duty; T dependability

---

ACTIVITY 43

ABOUT AS SMART AS CARRYING A JACKASS UPSIDE DOWN

An Aesop Fable retold

Donkeys are beasts of burden, nature made them that way,
That's why the farmer and his son took their donkey with them that day.
They were off to market to get some things for which they had need,
You know, things like flour, a little bacon, a few tools and some seed.

The day was bright and sunny, the air was crisp and clear,
And as they walked to town, their hearts were filled with cheer.
This was a day they had long looked forward to,
For going to market wasn't something they often got to do.

But along the way some girls pointed and giggled at the farmer and his son,
"Have you ever seen such fools, walking with a donkey instead of riding?" said one.
Well, the farmer and his son were ordinary people, pretty much like you and me,
They didn't like to be called fools, that's not something they wanted to be.

So the farmer said, "Get on the donkey my boy, and you can ride to town."
"We're not fools." he thought, as his smile became a frown.
Obediently, the boy climbed on, and they resumed their journey,
And before long their cheer returned, for the day was bright and sunny.

That is until they saw some old men, just sitting in the sun and talking,
And, one of them shouted, "See that boy riding while his father's walking.
"It's like I told you," the old man said, "There's no respect for age.
"That boy'll grow up worthless. I'd bet my yearly wage. "

Startled, the farmer and his son looked into their faces,
 "It would look better, I suppose," the farmer sighed, "if you and I traded places."
So with a frown on his face, the farmer got up after his son got down
And the three resumed their journey to the market in the town.

Just as their cheer was starting to return, they came upon some country women,
Sitting in the shade while sewing and chatting and watching their children.
But, as they came into view, the women were outraged, "You lazy old scamp!" they cried,
"How can you make that child walk while you sit on the donkey and ride?"

Not wanting to be thought lazy, the farmer said, "Jump up behind me boy."
And shortly they came to the edge of town, but by now, the trip had lost its joy.
Then suddenly a townsman shouted, "Have you no shame, overloading that beast as you do?
Why, the two of you could more easily carry that donkey than it carry the likes of you."

"Well, let's get off, there's only one thing left," sighed the farmer with a frown,
"You and I will have to pick up this donkey and carry it into town."
So they picked up the poor creature and put it on their shoulders with its feet pointing in the air.
"Don't worry son," the farmer said, "we just have to cross the bridge and shortly we'll be there."

By the time they reached the bridge a large crowd had gathered from town,
To see man and a boy carrying a donkey on their shoulders upside down,
Then as the three started across the bridge, the donkey tried to turn upright,
Throwing them all into the water, as everyone watched with sheer delight.

Well, as you might guess, the farmer and his son felt very foolish that day,
To end up in the water with their donkey that way.
So remember, that yielding to peer pressure, as tempting as it may seem,
Is about as smart as carrying a jackass, upside down, across a muddy stream.

Hindsight Questions:
• What were some of the different choices the farmer and his son made?

Insight Questions:
• Who controlled the choices the farmer and his son made?
• What is the risk in making choices based on other people's opinions?
• What were the farmer and his son missing?

Foresight Questions:
• What could the farmer and his son have done to avoid the problems they got into?

Discussion Opportunity: Iwannit Now convinced the farmer and his son it was important to have the approval of others. Biggs Bigger made the most recent opinion seem more important than the previous opinion. Unfortunately, the two never took ownership of their own opinions and did not exercise the internal control necessary for making good choices. Character Traits: RO ownership; T dependable

ACTIVITY 44

ROBINSON CRUSOE EXPOSTULATES T'OTHER WAY

From Daniel DeFoe's *Robinson Crusoe*

Introduce this reading by explaining that, as a young man, Robinson Crusoe decided not to pursue the profession his father had selected for him and chose instead to become a seaman. On one of his voyages, he became shipwrecked and stranded on an isolated island. Of all of his shipmates, he was the only one to survive. The following excerpt describes how he felt about his new circumstances.

Having now fixed my habitation, I found it absolutely necessary to provide a place to make a fire, and fuel to burn; and what I did for that, as also how I enlarged my cave, and what conveniences I made, I shall give a full account of in its place. But I must first give some little account of myself, and of my thoughts about living, which it may well be supposed were not a few.

I had a dismal prospect of my condition; for as I was not cast away upon that island without being driven, as is said, by a violent storm, quite out of the course or our intended voyage, and a great way, viz., some hundreds of leagues out of the ordinary course of the trade of mankind. I had great reason to consider it as a determination of Heaven, that in this desolate place, and in this desolate manner, I should end my life. The tears would run plentifully down my face when I made these reflections, and sometimes I would expostulate with myself, why Providence, should thus completely ruin it's creatures, and render them so absolutely miserable, so without help abandoned, so entirely depressed, that it could hardly be rational to be thankful for such a life.

But something always returned swift upon me to check these thoughts, and to reprove me; and particularly one day, walking with my gun in my hand by the seaside, I was very pensive upon the subject of my present condition, when Reason, as it were, expostulated with me t'other way, thus: "Well, you are in a desolate condition, it is true, but pray remember, where are the rest of you? Did you not come eleven of you into the boat? Where are the ten? Why were they not saved and you lost? Why were you singled out? Is it better to be here or there?" And then I pointed to the sea. All

evils are to be considered with the good that is in them, and with what worse attends them.

Then it occurred to me again, how I was furnished for my subsistence, and what would have been my case if it had not happened, which was an hundred thousand to one, that the ship floated from the place where she first struck and was driven so near to the shore that I had time to get all these things out of her; what would have been my case, if I had to have lived in the condition in which I at first came on shore, without the necessaries of life, or the means to supply and procure them? "Particularly," said I aloud (though to myself), "what should I have done without a gun, without ammunition, without any tools to make anything or to work with, without clothes, bedding, a tent, or any manner of covering?" and that now I had all these to a sufficient quantity, and was in a fair way to provide myself in such a manner, as to live without my gun when my ammunition was spent; so that I had a tolerable view of subsisting without any want as long as I lived. . . .

I now began to consider seriously my condition, and the circumstances I was reduced to; and I drew up the state of my affairs in writing. . . .And as my reason began now to master my despondency, I began to comfort myself as well as I could, and to set the good against the evil, that I might have something to distinguish my case from worse; and I stated it very impartially, like debtor and creditor, the comforts I enjoyed against the miseries I suffered, thus:

Upon the whole, here was an undoubted testimony, that there was scarce any situation in the world so miserable, but there was something. . . . to be thankful for in it. . .

Evil	Good
I am cast upon a horrible desolate island void of all hope of recovery.	But I am alive, and not drowned, as all my ship's company was.
I am singled out and separated, as it were, from all the world to be miserable.	But I am singled out, too, from all the ship's crew to be spared from death;
I am divided from mankind, a solitaire, one banished from human society.	But I am not starved and perishing on a barren place affording no sustenance.
I have not clothes to cover me.	But I am in a hot climate, where if I had clothes I could hardly wear them.
I am without any defense or means to resist any violence of man or beast.	But I am cast on an island where I see no wild beasts to hurt me, as I saw on the coast of Africa; what if I had been shipwrecked there?
I have no soul to speak to or relieve me.	But God so wonderfully sent the ship in near enough to the shore, that I have gotten out so many necessary things [to] supply my wants.

Hindsight Questions
- What were Robinson Crusoe's first thoughts upon finding himself stranded and alone?
- What did Crusoe choose to think instead?

Insight Questions
- What did it take for Crusoe to gain control of his thoughts?
- How is his story an example of the C skill of Correction?

Foresight Questions
- What was Crusoe's technique for sorting out his thoughts and feelings?
- How could you apply this technique in your own life?
- Why is it helpful to try to find the good in any situation we may find ourselves?

Discussion Opportunity: Robinson Crusoe was in a bad fix. He was alone and stranded. In this condition, the Stink'n Think'n Gang tried to get the best of him. Biggs Bigger tried to make his problems seem unbearable, while Eency Weency Tiny Too tried to make him think there was nothing good in his situation. The Seven C Skills came to his rescue, however. Control enabled him to keep his feelings in check. Curiosity caused him to wonder if perhaps there weren't something good about his circumstances. Concentration and Criticism helped him look more closely at the good and evil in his situation. Creativity helped him find a way of making the comparisons, and Correction gave him the ability to change the way he was thinking. Through it all, Communication helped him use his self-talking skills to his advantage. Character Traits: RO ownership; SR self-reliance

To reinforce the lesson in this story and to provide a practical example of how students can apply it in their lives, invite your students to take a situation in their lives they are not happy about and use this method of reasoning to see if they can find the good in it. Have them take a sheet of paper and list on it the things they don't like about the situation. Then have them prepare a list of the good they can find or the things they can learn or gain from the situation.

ACTIVITY 45

PAPER BAG PUPPET READINGS

ADVANCE PREPARATION: *Photocopy the following readings and cut out a reading to give to each student along with a paper lunch bag. Also needed are construction paper, scissors, glue, and crayons.*

Have each student make a paper bag puppet representing the animal he or she received and glue the reading on the back. Have them stand in a circle with their puppets and read the reading for that puppet. Explain that each paired statement represents two different ways of looking at the same situation.

1. I'm a poor little mouse that has no house,
   Poor, poor me.

   But out in the field, I'm free as can be,
   Hi diddle, Hay diddle, Hi dee.

2. I'm a poor little kitten that's lost it's mitten,
   Poor, poor me.

   But without my mitten, I can climb up a tree,
   Hi diddle, Hay diddle, Hi dee.

3. I'm a poor little dog that lives in a log,
   Poor, poor me.

   But the log where I live keeps the rain off of me,
   Hi diddle, Hay diddle, Hi dee.

4. I'm a poor little duck that's down on her luck,
   Poor, poor me.

   But I can quack with the best as you can see,
   Hi diddle, Hay diddle, Hi dee.

5. I'm a poor little deer that's running in fear,
   Poor, poor me.

   But I can run fast, as fast as can be,
   Hi diddle, Hay diddle, Hi dee.

6. I'm a poor little fox that's too big for a box,
   Poor, poor me.

   But a fox in a box would be silly to see,
   Hi diddle, Hay diddle, Hi dee.

7. I'm a poor little bear with too much hair,
   Poor, poor me.

   But I sleep through the winter warm as can be,
   Hi diddle, Hay diddle, Hi dee.

8. I'm a poor little goat that fell out of a boat,
   Poor, poor me.

   But I got a fine bath and I'm clean you see,
   Hi diddle, Hay diddle, Hi dee.

9. I'm a poor little pig that's not very big,
   Poor, poor me.

   But I'm too little to eat, that's fine with me,
   Hi diddle, Hay diddle, Hi dee.

10. I'm a poor rabbit that has a bad habit,
    Poor, poor me.

    But if I kick that bad habit, then I'll be free,
    Hi diddle, Hay diddle, Hi dee.

11. I'm a poor little frog that lives in a bog,
    Poor, poor me.

    But I've plenty to eat as you can see,
    Hi diddle, Hay diddle, Hi dee.

12. I'm a poor little fish that lives in a bowl,
    Poor, poor me.

    But from my bowl there's lots I can see,
    Hi diddle, Hay diddle, Hi dee.

13. I'm a poor little worm that has to squirm,
    Poor, poor me.

    But if I had legs, I wouldn't be me,
    Hi diddle, Hay diddle, Hi dee.

14. I'm a poor little chick that's feeling sick,
    Poor, poor me.

    But I get to stay home and watch the TV,
    Hi diddle, Hay diddle, Hi dee.

15. I'm a poor little bird that can't be heard,
    Poor, poor me.

    But my song's prettiest of any bird in the tree,
    Hi diddle, Hay diddle, Hi dee.

Hindsight Questions
- What was the first thought each of these puppet animals had?
- What was the second thought?

Insight Questions
- How was the ability to Control their thoughts helpful to them?
- How did each of these puppets use the C skill of Correction?

Foresight Questions
- Why is it helpful to be able to see the good when things aren't going well?

Discussion Opportunity: Things weren't going well for these puppets. But each was able to take ownership of its thoughts and feelings and look for something good in its situation. The Stink'n Think'n Gang will try to make you feel sorry for yourself. But the Seven C Skills can help you gain control of your thoughts and get them turned around. This is an example of Correction. Character Traits: PR ownership

---

ACTIVITY 46

THE FARMER AND HIS DAME

by George L. Rogers

There's an old, old story told
Of a farmer and his dame,
Frederick he was called
and Liesel was her name.

Rosalie was their daughter,
Of children they had one,
But she was quick and lively,
And, hulla ho, how she could run.

With them lived their dog named Fritz,
Of animals, they had twenty.
With two milk cows, two sheep, two sows,
Their thirteen geese were plenty.

Frederick worked hard each day:
Sowing seeds
Hoeing weeds
Milking cows
Fencing sows
Shearing fleece
And feeding geese,
Not to mention, cutting hay.

And Liesel worked just as hard:
Mending clothes
Tending Rose
Baking bread
Spinning thread
Cleaning house
And feeding spouse,
Not to mention, rending lard.

But Frederick somehow had it in his mind,
That he worked hardest of the two.
"Be glad your work is easy" Frederick said,
"And none too hard to do."

"My work's none too easy," Liesel said,
"Tomorrow let's make a test.
I'll do your work and you do mine,
Then we'll see whose work is best"

So early morn in cool of day,
Liesel rose and milked the cow,
She fed the stock and did the chores,
Then off she went to plow.

Frederick thought he'd sleep awhile,
But soon was pulled from bed.
Rosalie was getting hungry,
And she wanted to be fed.

"Ah, we'll have some bacon!" Frederick thought.
"That sounds mighty good."
So he put the bacon in a pan
And went to get some wood.

But when Frederick came back in the house,
Fritz ran out the door,
He had the bacon in his mouth,
And, hula ho, there was no more.

"Well, bread and milk will have to do,"
Said Frederick to himself,
But when he went to get the bread,
There was none upon the shelf.

"Then, I'll make some bread." he thought.
"That's really not so hard."
So he ground some grain to make the flour,
And melted down some lard.

But while Frederick was busy making bread,
Rosalie ran out to play,
And before he knew what happened,
Was in a terrible fray.

Rosalie had opened the barnyard gate,
All the animals had left their pen,
Now they were free and running loose,
And Fritz was chasing after them.

Frederick ran out to stop the ruckus,
But forgot to close the door,
Soon pigs and geese were in the house,
Spilling milk and flour upon the floor.

When Liesel returned from work that night,
She found a frazzled spouse,
Holding a crying child and chasing pigs,
Around a messy house.

"Nay Liesel, your work 'tis none too easy,"
Said Frederick to his dame.
"So tomorrow I'll work the field,
If to you it's just the same."

Hindsight Questions
- What happened when Frederick tried to do Liesel's work?
- What did Frederick find out about Liesel's work?

Insight Questions
- Why did Frederick think his job was harder than Liesel's before they changed places?
- Which of the Stink'n Think'n Gang influenced Frederick?
- How can new knowledge and experiences lead us to change our viewpoints?

Foresight Questions
- Why is it important to be open to new knowledge and to learn from our experiences?

Discussion Opportunity: Judge B Fore tried to convince Frederick his job was harder than Liesel's. Biggs Bigger and Eency Weency Tiny Too added their influence But Frederick changed his viewpoint when they changed jobs for a day. Frederick's experience taught him that he had underestimated the difficulty of Liesel's work and undervalued its importance. It also taught him that he had overvalued the importance of his own work. He went back into the field as a humbler and wiser man. In taking greater ownership of his thoughts and feelings, Frederick developed greater responsibility for how he looked at their situation. Character Traits: PR ownership; SR self-understanding

---

CHOOSING TO BE RESPONSIBLE

Section Three

❧

LEARNING OBJECTIVES FOR SECTION THREE

Understand the four elements of Personal Responsibility

The Ability to Act

The Right to Act

The Duty to Act, and

Accountability for Acting

Take ownership of thoughts and feelings (attitudes)

Take ownership of choices and actions

SECTION OVERVIEW

The Annual Report to the Board of Overseers of Harvard University on January 11, 1943 stated that "The primary concern of American education today is. . . .to cultivate in the largest possible number of our future citizens an appreciation of both the responsibilities and the benefits which come to them because they are Americans and are free."

As Americans, we frequently concern ourselves with the rights of citizenship and are quick to claim its benefits. But just as frequently we fail to concern ourselves with its responsibilities. Yet, the freedoms we so highly prize are entirely dependent on the responsible exercise of the rights we claim. As Benjamin Franklin wrote, "Only a virtuous people are capable of freedom. As nations become corrupt and vicious, they have more need of masters."

Responsibility is about taking ownership of our choices and actions, it consists of the ability to act, the right to act, the duty to act, and accepting accountability.

The Ability to Act

Each of us is an independent agent, capable of causing things to happen, both good and bad. How we choose to use this ability determines the course of our lives and the kind of people we become. This ability is unique to each person and is the direct result of the connection between an individual's brain and his or her body.

The Right to Act

The ability to act does not confer the right to act. There are many things we are able to do that we have no right to do. The Declaration of Independence proclaims that life, liberty, and the pursuit of happiness is a universal right. As such, each of us has the right to preserve and pursue these rights for ourselves and loved ones. But we can only do so in a manner that does not deny these same rights to anyone else.

The Duty to Act

Personal responsibility largely consists of obligations or duties imposed upon us by the very nature of our own existence. The obligation to choose what we believe, to decide how we will act, and to determine what we will become can never be escaped, ignored, or delegated without penalty. No one else can think what we think, feel what we feel, believe what we believe, or do what we do.

In addition, when others are dependent on us and we are in positions of trust, we have the duty to act in a manner that will justify that trust.

Accepting Accountability

Having granted us the ability and right to think and act for ourselves nature, in turn, holds us answerable for our use of this capacity. We are also answerable to others when we violate their rights.

Thus it is, that only by taking personal ownership of our thoughts, feelings, and actions are we ever able to achieve our full potential.

ACTIVITY 47

CULTURAL QUILT

ADVANCE PREPARATION: *Have students bring copies of magazines with pictures of people from around the world. Also needed are scissors, glue, and construction paper.*

Have students cut out pictures illustrating how people in different countries and places eat, sleep, work and play, along with pictures of their housing, transportation, clothing and other scenes representative of these countries and cultures.

To make a cultural quilt, have your students paste these pictures on colored construction paper then put the pictures next to each other on the classroom wall. Explore with your students how people are influenced in what they wear, what they eat, where they go, and how they make a living by where they live.

Hindsight Questions
- How are the people in these pictures like you?
- How are they different?

Insight Questions
- How does where you live influence what you eat? What you wear? Where you sleep? Where you go to school? etc.
- How does where you live influence what you think is important?

Foresight Questions
- As you get older, how much choice will you have in deciding where you live?
- How much choice will you have in deciding what kind of person you want to be?

Discussion Opportunity: Our external surroundings have a big influence on what we think and how we feel about things. It can also influence what we think is important and the choices we make. Iwannit Now uses our external environment to get us to want things that may not be good for us. He can be very successful in getting us to think we can't get by without the things our friends have. Only by gaining internal control and taking ownership of our thoughts and feelings can we escape the influences of the Stink'n Think'n Gang. Character Traits: PR ownership; RO citizenship

---

ACTIVITY 48

FROG PANTOMIMES

For each of the following, invite a student to pantomime the situation and have the rest of the class guess at what the student is doing with a frog.

1. A person trying to catch a frog.
2. A person trying to train a frog to jump in a race.
3. A person eating frog legs who likes them.
4. A scientist cutting open a dead frog to study its parts.

After the activity, ask by a raise of hands, who would like to (catch, train, eat, or dissect) frogs? Why? Explain that the differences in raised hands represent different mental positions or attitudes. Some people like to catch frogs, others can't stand the idea of even touching one. Some people like to eat frog legs, other's can't stand the thought. A scientist who studies the parts of a frog to understand how its bones and muscles are connected might not have the slightest interest in training a frog, while someone who trains frogs may dislike the idea of ever dissecting one.

Hindsight Questions
* What different viewpoints did class members have about catching frogs?
* What different viewpoints did class members have about eating frog legs?

Insight Questions
* What determines a person's desire to catch frogs?
* Why might a person choose to eat frog legs for the first time?
* Why do different people sometimes choose to look at the same thing in different ways?

Foresight Questions
* How can understanding your own attitude help you in making choices?
* How can understanding different viewpoints help you in making choices?
* How do these ideas apply to more serious topics like using drugs?

Discussion Opportunity: Different people often look at things differently. Some can't tolerate the idea of eating frog legs while others think they are delicious. Some have difficulty with cutting open a frog and looking at its parts, while others find it interesting. Different interests, different experiences, different personalities all combine to give us different viewpoints. These differences can be a source of strength, making it possible for us to learn from each other. The important thing to understand is that some viewpoints are more helpful than others and all viewpoints are not equal. The important thing is that we take ownership of our thoughts and feelings and make sure they are consistent with the nature of things. Character Traits: PR ownership; RO citizenship

---

ACTIVITY 49

THE SPOILED PRINCESS

by George L. Rogers

The King hated to admit it, but the Princess was spoiled. Spoiled rotten! From the day she was born till this very moment, the King made sure that whatever his royal offspring wanted, she got. It wasn't so much that the King was foolish. It's just that he wasn't always wise. And when it came to the Princess, it seemed that the King was seldom ever wise.

She was a pretty child, and he loved her greatly; so greatly that he could not stand to see her cry. The Princess learned very early that to get anything she wanted, all she had to do was cry. As things were, she wanted a lot, so she spent a great deal of time crying. As soon as she got one thing, she cried for another. Sometimes, she didn't even wait. Before her servants were on the way to get one thing, she began crying for another. Day by day, the rooms, closets, and storage areas in the castle were filled to overflowing with things the Princess wanted.

Although the King was concerned about all of the things the Princess was accumulating, that was not his greatest concern. No, to him, the big problem was much different. The Princess had simply become insufferable to be around. She was the center of the universe as far as she was concerned. All others were there simply to meet her wishes. She had her servants running day and night, commanding them to do this or to get that. When she went for rides in the royal carriage, she had her drivers run anyone off the road who got in their way. Peasants on their way to market with a few eggs to sell, or perhaps a load of wood, would be run off the road, breaking eggs, and dumping wood all over. The princess would simply say, "They should know to get out of the way when we are coming."

When dignitaries came to visit the King, the Princess would invariably and rudely interrupt the proceedings to insist that she get something or other. Even the King, it seemed, had no other role than to provide for her wants.

The King asked himself over and over, "What to do?" "What to do?" So, he called in his advisors to ask them what he should do. After much discussion, they advised the King to invite several children to the castle each day to play with the princess. This they said would help her to make friends and learn to share. The King agreed, and children were invited. The experiment did not prove successful, however. Rather than learning to share, the Princess simply saw her new playmates as so many additional servants. They had to play the games she wanted to play and she would only allow them to do the things she wanted to do. If anyone protested, she had them banished from the court, and they were sent home never again to return. Before long, no children were left for the princess to play with.

The King was beside himself. "What to do? What to do?" the King asked himself, again and again. Once more, he convened his council of advisors and one more time they pondered the problem. This time, they advised the King, he should send the Princess on a one year tour of other countries and places. This, they said would give her experience, and would help her to appreciate all the interesting people, places, and things there are in the world. The King was delighted. "Surely this will work he thought." So off the Princess went, to learn what she would learn.

Finally the time came for the Princess to return. The King was anxious to hear of her experiences and to see the change that had taken place. When the Princess returned she did not have one good word to say about any place she had been, food she had eaten, or person she had met. The cities were dirty, the countryside was boring. People she met were either stupid, odd or incompetent. As for the food, she had only one word, "disgusting."

By night fall, the King was pacing the floor, saying over and over again, "What to do? What to do? What to do?"

Group discussion - *With your students consider:*
- What will happen if the King does nothing?
- What is the biggest problem the Princess has?
- What do you think the King should do?
- How would you write the ending to this story?

Now read the ending to the story.

The King truly loved his daughter, but he realized that unless she changed, he might well be the only person who ever would. He therefore decided upon drastic action. And while he was not always a wise King, neither was he always foolish. The King told the princess plainly of his concerns. He explained that he must take away her royal possessions and send her to live among the peasants. She was to eat as they ate, work as they worked, and to wear what they wore.

Such was his love for his daughter, the King also decided that, one day of every ten, he too would spend among the peasants, working, eating, and living as they did.

Well, as you might guess, the princess did not respond very well to the King's decision. But he was still King and in this instance was firm in his resolve. At first the Princess expected everyone to wait on her as in the past, but when she became hungry she learned she had to get food for herself. Sometimes, she discovered the peasants did not always have enough food to eat. She also learned what it was like to work all day in the fields and to fall in bed exhausted in the evening. In time the Princess came to know and like the peasants with whom she lived and worked. For the first time in her life, she really had friends.

The King too, learned many things about the hardships his people faced. He began to realize that he had not always been a good King. He discovered that it is a poor satisfaction to think of yourself as a wise and powerful ruler, when everyone else thinks of you as foolish and weak.

In his remaining years the King made many improvements in how he ruled his people. He enacted better laws and executed better judgment in the affairs of the kingdom than he had ever done before.

In time the Princess returned to claim the throne of her father when he died. She became known as "Princess the Beloved." For by knowing her people and understanding both their needs and their potential, she was able to be the finest monarch her country had ever known.

Hindsight Questions
- How did Iwannit Now influence choices the Princesses made?
- How happy did getting the things she wanted make her?

Insight Questions
- When did the Princess finally take ownership for her thoughts and feelings?
- How did this prove to be an advantage to her?

Foresight Questions
- Why is it sometimes important to curb our wants?

ACTIVITY 50

MAC AND ZACH FROM HACKENSACK

by George L. Rogers

To the family of Black in Hackensack
Were born twin sons named Mac and Zach.

Now Mac and Zach were normal boys
Who loved to play with friends and toys,
Who loved to roam the great outdoors,
And play fun games on mother's floors.

But these two boys from Hackensack
Were not the same, this Zach and Mac.
For Zach was short and Mac was tall,
And Mac was large where Zach was small.

Where Mac was talented, quick, and bright,
Zach had trouble in doing things right.
And where Mac did well in school and sports,
Zach had problems of many sorts.

In choosing up sides to play any game,
For these two boys, it was always the same.
First would be Mac, last would be Zach,
And that's how it was in Hackensack.

Now tell me quick in voices low,
From what you've heard and what you know,
Of these two boys from Hackensack,
The boy named Mac or his brother Zach,
Who do you think is happiest now?
Give me the whatfor, the whyfor and how.?
(*Discuss the first set of questions on page 81*)

If one's talents were the only test
By which to judge who lives the best,
Mac, not Zach, would be most glad,
And Zach, not Mac, the one most sad.

But in the larger scheme of life,
With all its challenge toil and strife,

The scales most tipped by attitude,
And not its cousin aptitude.

You see, Mac was a boy who liked to be first,
And when he wasn't, it brought out his worst.
For Mac was not a patient lad,
And what he wanted, he wanted bad.

He wanted it quick, he wanted it now,
No matter the who, no matter the how.
"I want what I want when I want it!" he'd say,
"I'll never be happy until I get my own way."

Well as you might guess, more often than not,
The thing Mac wanted, he never got.
And oh my! How the sparks would fly,
You'd think the poor boy was about to die.

But with Zach, things were different for him,
With his twinkling eyes, and cheerful grin.
For slow as he was, there some things he knew
By figuring them out and thinking them through.

Zach knew:
You can never enjoy being somewhere you're not,
Nor something you want, but haven't got.
You can never enjoy doing a thing you can't do,
Anymore than you can be someone other than you.

So Zach did something remarkable for such a
    young lad,
He decided to be happy with who he was and
    what he had.

And it was remarkable what Zachary could do,
With a little string, some cardboard, and glue.
So the forts and castles he did build,
Kept his hands busy and kept his hours filled.

Zach didn't need to have the last say.
He didn't worry whether he got his own way.
He enjoyed the snow, he enjoyed the sun,
He enjoyed his friends and having fun.
Whether fielder or batter, his or their toy,
They were all there for Zach to enjoy.

Now tell me quick in voices low,
From what you've heard and what you know,
Of these two boys from Hackensack,
The boy named Mac or his brother Zach,
Who do you think is happiest now?
Give me the whatfor, the whyfor, and how?
(Discuss the second set of questions on page 81)

Illustration by Stefanie Eskander

First Set of Questions

Hindsight Questions
* In what ways are Mac and Zach physically different?
* How much choice did they have in these differences?

Second Set of Questions

Hindsight Questions
* How are Mac and Zach different in how they think and feel?
* How did this influence their choices?

Insight Questions
* How much choice did they have in these differences?
* How much ownership was Mac taking of his thoughts and feelings?

Foresight Questions
* Which differences do you think will make the greatest difference in their lives, physical or mental?

Discussion Opportunity: How people think and feel about themselves and others (attitude) is far more important than natural talents and abilities (aptitudes) they are born with. People who always want things their own way are sure to be disappointed much of the time. Iwannit Now had a great hold on Mac. Though he had many reasons to be happy, he generally chose to be miserable. Zach, on the other hand, may have had reasons to be miserable, but he chose to be happy. Mac did not take ownership of his thoughts and feelings or of his choices. Character Traits: PR duty; SR self-understanding; RO caring

ACTIVITY 51

THE LESSON OF THE SECRET GARDEN

From *The Secret Garden* by Francis Hodgson Burnett

In each century since the beginning of the world, wonderful things have been discovered. In the last century more amazing things were found out than in any century before. In this new century hundreds of things still more astounding will be brought to light. At first people refuse to believe that a strange new thing can be done, then they begin to hope it can be done, then they see it can be done—then it is done and all the world wonders why it was not done centuries before.

One of the new things people began to find out in the last century was that thoughts—just mere thoughts—are as powerful as electric batteries—as good for one as sunlight is, or as bad for one as poison. To let a sad thought or a bad thought get into your mind is as dangerous as letting a scarlet fever germ get into your body. If you let it stay there after it has got in, you may never get over it as long as you live.

So long as Mistress Mary's mind was full of disagreeable thoughts about her dislikes and sour opinions of people and her determination not to be pleased by or interested in anything, she was a yellow-faced, sickly, bored and wretched child. Circumstances, however, were very kind to her, though she was not at all aware of it. They began to push her about for her own good. When [she entered the secret garden and] her mind gradually filled itself with robins, and moorland cottages crowded with children, with queer crabbed old gardeners and common little Yorkshire house maids, with springtime and with secret gardens coming alive day by day, and also with a moor boy and his "creatures," there was no room left for the disagreeable thoughts that affected her liver and her digestion and made her yellow and tired.

So long as Colin shut himself up in his room and thought only of his fears and weakness and his dislike of people who looked at him and reflected hourly on humps and early death, he was a hysterical, half-crazy little hypochondriac who knew nothing of the sunshine and the spring, and also did not know that he could get well and stand upon his feet if he tried to do it. [But in the secret garden] when new beautiful thoughts began to push out the old hideous ones, life began to come back to him, his blood ran healthily through his veins and strength poured into him like a flood. His scientific experiment was quite practical and simple and there was nothing weird about it at all. Much more surprising things can happen to anyone who, when a disagreeable or discouraged thought comes into his mind, just has the sense to remember in time and push it out by putting in an agreeable, determinedly courageous one. Two things cannot be in the same place at the same time.

"Where you tend a rose, my lad, A thistle cannot grow."

Hindsight Questions
- What kind of thoughts filled Mistress Mary's mind before the Secret Garden?
- How did they make her feel? What about Colin?
- What did Mary and Colin learn in the Secret Garden?

Insight Questions
- How much choice was involved in their making the change?
- What does the quote about the thistle and the rose mean?
- What kind of effort does it take to push out a disagreeable thought with an agreeable one?

Foresight Questions
- How can replacing disagreeable thoughts with more agreeable ones be helpful to you?
- What can you do to think more agreeable thoughts?

Discussion Opportunity: The mind is always filled with some kind of thoughts. It is up to us to choose which kinds of thoughts we wish to fill it with. If we choose to just let our minds drift without guidance, they will be filled with aimless, wandering thoughts. Mor e often than not, such thoughts tend to dwell on the unpleasant. But we can all have our secret garden if we want. We can plant it in our minds by looking for the good things around us and learning to appreciate them. The Stink'n Think'n Gang will try to keep you from it, but if you choose to develop the seven C skills you can overcome their influence. Character Traits: PR duty, ownership; SR self-reliance

---

ACTIVITY 52

WHAT DOES IT MEAN?

Divide class into small groups to discuss the meaning of one or more of the following statements. Younger students will need some explanations of what they mean.

"The unexamined life is not worth living."
Socrates

"As we all wish to live, we are obligated by reason to take as much care for our future as our present happiness and not build one on the ruins of the other."
Benjamin Franklin

"Not enjoyment, and not sorrow,
Is our destined end or way;
But to act that each tomorrow
Finds us further than today."
Henry Wadsworth Longfellow

Hindsight Questions
- What did you learn from discussing this quote?

Insight Questions
- What is required of you to do what the quote suggests?

Foresight Questions
- How would doing that be to your advantage?

BIOGRAPHY

MICHAEL'S SPEECH

The audience was angry. The man speaking to them had just spent ten minutes telling them how fortunate they were. He had criticized them for self-pity and told them they had no reason to feel sorry for themselves. Who was he to talk to them like that? Every person in the room had recently lost an arm or a leg from exploding land mines and enemy mortar. Some had other serious injuries as well. Most had only recently returned from the front lines where two armies were desperately locked in a life and death struggle. What did this man know of their suffering? What right did he have to stand in front of them and criticize them for feeling as they did?

Sensing their anger, the speaker moved toward the audience, increasing the severity of his criticism. There were boos and hisses from the audience. As he moved down the aisle, continuing his speech, the audience became furious and some started jeering.

Unexpectedly, the speaker stopped talking. He pulled a chair into the aisle, and sat down. Without saying a word, he carefully removed one of his legs. A sudden hush came over the audience. Next, the man slowly and deliberately removed his other leg. There was a large gasp from the crowd. Then, to their utter amazement, the speaker removed one of his arms. By this time, there was dead silence in the hall. Finally, he removed several parts from his other hand and sat before the audience, just the stump of a man remaining. The speaker, Michael J. Dowling, had just demonstrated that even a person who has suffered serious injuries has choices. Choices about how to look at things. Choices about how to approach life.

At the age of 14, Michael was caught in a blizzard and suffered extreme frostbite. To save his life, doctors amputated both legs, one arm, and much of his remaining hand. But Michael was a determined young man. He went on to pursue successful careers in education, business, and politics and to raise a family of three children. Much of his later life was spent giving motivational speeches to disabled war veterans during World War I.

Hindsight Questions
- How did the soldiers feel about their injuries?
- Why were they angry with Michael?

Insight Questions
- Why did the soldier's attitudes change when Michael took off his legs?
- How might a person's attitude prove to be a greater disability than an injury to the body?

Foresight Questions
- What choices did Michael have to make after he lost his legs, arm, and some of his other hand?
- Why is it important to take ownership of your thoughts and feelings in making choices?

Discussion Opportunity: Michael recognized that to have any quality of life, he had to take ownership of his thoughts, feelings, and choices. He had wanted to feel sorry for himself, but he used Concentration, Control, and Correction and chose instead to make something of his life. In doing so, he became a far happier person and helped others as well. Character Traits: PR own; SR self-understanding

ACTIVITY 54

DADDY DEAR

by George L. Rogers

Assign two students to read this story to the class. Photocopy the story for each reader. You may wish to have your students make two paper plate puppets, one for Daddy Dear and one for Daughter Jean.

Jean: Daddy dear, may I get a puppy, pretty please?
Father: Daughter, you may have a puppy if you please.
          But if you get a puppy, daughter Jean,
          You must feed it, and walk it, and keep it clean.

Father: Wiggles' bowls are empty, daughter Jean,
          Will you give him water and meat that's lean?
Jean: Do I really have to, Daddy dear?
          Wiggle's out there and I'm in here.
          What I'm doing now is such great fun!
          Can't feeding Wiggles wait until I'm done?

Father: Wiggles needs his walk now, daughter Jean
          Will you walk him down to Briar's Green?
Jean: Do I really have to, Daddy dear?
          Walking Wiggles there is not real near.
          And can't you see I'm not real keen,
          To watch Wiggles waddle down to Briar's Green?

Father: Wiggles made a puddle, daughter Jean.
          Will you get a rag and wipe it clean?
Jean: Do I really have to, Daddy dear?
          Wiping Wiggles' puddles makes me queer!
          It makes me sick and makes me gag,
          To wipe Wiggles' puddles with an old cloth rag.

Hindsight Questions
* What three things is Jean supposed to do for Wiggles?

Insight Questions
* Why are these her jobs to do?
* Why are these three things important for her to do?

Foresight Questions
* What will happen if she does not do them?

Discussion Opportunity: Jean wanted the fun of a puppy but not the daily duties. A puppy has many needs. Part of caring for a puppy is feeding it, walking it, and cleaning up after it. Iwannit Now convinced Jean she wanted a puppy. Biggs Bigger made it very important to her. And Eency Weency Tiny Too minimized the work necessary to take care of Wiggles. For Jean to really take ownership of her choice to get a puppy, she will have to accept her duty to take care of Wiggles. Character Traits: RO duty

ACTIVITY 55

ABC SEQUENCE

55-1 ——————————— Tennis Ball Demo ———————————

ADVANCE PREPARATION: *This activity requires three tennis balls marked "A," "B," and "C."*

Place the three tennis balls on a table. Explain that the "A" ball represents attitudes, the "B" ball represents behavior, and the "C" ball represents consequences. Roll the "A" ball into the "B" ball so that the "B" ball hits the "C" ball. If you do it so the "C" ball rolls off the table, it will give the demonstration some additional dramatic effect. You may have to practice this a couple of times before you can do it just right.

Explain that attitudes influence behaviors and behaviors cause consequences. We can control our attitudes and behaviors, but we cannot control consequences. The best point of control is our attitudes.

55-2 ——————————— ABC Chalk Talk ———————————

A chalk talk matching specific attitudes to specific behaviors and consequences may be helpful in reinforcing the tennis ball demo. Just put a couple of simple examples relevant to your students' experiences on the chalkboard—for example, a person's attitude toward water.

ABC CHALK TALK		
Attitude About water	**Behavior**	**Consequence**
Afraid of water	Stay away from water Don't learn to swim	Not able to enjoy water sports, unable to swim if need ever arose, at risk of drowning.
Enjoy water	Go near water whenever possible, learn to swim, water ski, etc.	Enjoy water sports swimming, boating, etc., safe around water

Hindsight Questions
- What did you learn from the ABC sequence?

Insight Questions
- What is the connection between attitudes, behaviors, and consequences?
- Of the three, which do you have the ability to choose?
- Of the three, which will give you the greatest control over the outcome?

Foresight Questions
- Why is it important to consider consequences before choosing any action?

Discussion Opportunity: We can control our behavior and actions. We can also control our thoughts and feelings (attitude). What we cannot control is the consequences or results of our actions. Since our actions are controlled by our attitudes, being able to control our thoughts and feelings gives us the greatest control over the results of our choices. When we are careless in forming our attitudes and do not take ownership of our thoughts and feelings, the Stink'n Think'n Gang can get us to believe and do many foolish things that produce unhappy consequences. Character Traits: RO accountability

---

ACTIVITY 56

WOULD YOU BELIEVE?

ADVANCE PREPARATION: *For each of the following stories, prepare overheads of the associated pictures on pages 93 and 94.*
Read the story, then place the overhead on the projector and ask, "What's wrong with this picture?"

56-1 ——————————————— Teresa's Tricycle ————————————

As Teresa hopped off her tricycle to play with her friends, she left it in the middle of the road. When one of her friends asked if she wanted to put her tricycle on the lawn, Teresa said, "No, it'll be just fine where it is."

Shortly, a car came along. When the car came to where the tricycle was parked, the car simply jumped over the tricycle. The driver, Mrs. McGee, was so delighted to have had such a fun experience, she stopped to thank Teresa for leaving her tricycle in the road.

A little later Teresa's mother came outside and saw where Teresa had left her tricycle. Just about that time a big truck came along. It too jumped over Teresa's tricycle. Teresa's mother thought it was such great fun to watch the truck jump over the tricycle, that she too was very happy Teresa had thought to leave her tricycle in the road. Of course, Teresa was very pleased with herself for having made such a good choice.

56-2 _____Grimey Griswold_____

Since Grimey Griswold did not like to work, he never had any money of his own. But for Grimey, this was not a problem. Every Monday morning at 9 am sharp, Grimey waited at the bank door with an empty wheelbarrow. When the bank opened for business, Grimey went inside and filled up his wheelbarrow with money from the bank's vault. He then took the money home and had enough to spend until the next Monday morning when he came back to the bank and got some more.

Grimey was one of the most respected citizens in Mayfield. He was a friendly thief and was on the best of terms with the bank president, the people who kept their money in the bank, and especially Charlie, the local police officer. No one minded his taking the money and Grimey lived very comfortably without working.

What's wrong with this picture?

Hindsight Questions
- What did (Teresa/Grimey) do? Why?

Insight Questions
- What's wrong with this story?

Foresight Questions
- What do you think would really happen?
- How would (Teresa's mother/the people who have money in the bank) really feel?

Discussion Opportunity: Teresa had a duty to take care of her tricycle. While she has the ability to leave it in the street, she does not have the right to do so. If she does leave it in the street and it gets hit by a car, she will not have a tricycle to ride. This is one way she will be made to answer for her choice. The bank officers and the police officer have a duty to protect the money in the bank from people like Grimey. Grimey does not have a right to the money in the bank. If he tries to take some, the police will try to catch him. If they do he will lose his freedom and perhaps his life. Others will try to make him answer for his crime. It is their duty. Character Traits: RO right, duty, accountability; RO citizenship; T honesty, dependability

---

ACTIVITY 57

THE TWO LITTLE PIGS

Once upon a time there were two little pigs. Although you may have heard there were three, I have it on good authority there were only two. It is possible, however, they were different pigs entirely, as in those days pigs were in great supply. Be that as it may, the two pigs decided to leave home and make their own way in the world. They needed a place to live and each decided to build a house. The first little was more interested in playing than building houses. So he built a straw house. Straw houses, you see, are quite easy to build. They don't take much time or work.

The second little pig, however, was more thoughtful. He knew that a brick house would last much longer and provide better protection than a house made of straw. So, though it took much longer, and was far more work, this little pig built his house with bricks.

Now, unbeknownst to the two little pigs, there lived a big bad wolf in the valley where they built their houses; a wolf who liked to eat little pigs for dinner. One evening, the big bad wolf knocked on the door of the little pig that had built his house of straw and said, "Little pig, little pig, let me come in."

Warily, the little pig looked out the window and seeing the wolf replied, "Not by the hair of my chinny, chin chin. I'll never, never let you in!"

"Very well then," said the wolf, "I will huff, and I will puff, and I will blow your house down." So the wolf huffed, and he puffed, and he puffed and he huffed until he blew the straw house down. But, before the wolf could catch its breath, the little pig took off and ran as fast as he could to the home of the little pig who had built his house of bricks.

The wolf was quick behind, however, and shortly after the little pig ran in the brick house, the big bad wolf knocked at the door.

"Little pigs, little pigs, let me come in," said the wolf.

"Not by the hair of our chinny, chin, chins." said the two little pigs, "We'll never, never let you in."

"Then I will huff, and I will puff, and I will blow the house down." said the wolf. And with that, the big bad wolf began huffing and puffing one more time. Well that poor old wolf, he huffed and he puffed, and he puffed and he huffed until he couldn't huff or puff anymore. But bad as he was, and puff as he might, the brick house would not blow down. It was built too strong. By this time the wolf was so blown out, he could no longer stand. So, before the wolf could regain his strength, the two little pigs scooped him into a wheelbarrow and took him off to the zoo where big bad wolves can get plenty to eat without frightening their neighbors.

Discussion Opportunity: Iwannit Now and Biggs Bigger will tell you play now and work later. But Criticism will tell you that you have a duty to take reasonable care for your own well-being. The little pig had a right to choose to build a straw house, but he also had a duty to build one that would give him adequate protection. The wolf did not have the right to blow down the little pig's straw house, but he did have the ability and chose to do so. The consequence was the pig lost his house and the wolf lost his freedom. Both were held answerable for their choices. Character Traits: RO duty; SR self-reliance, RO citizenship

ACTIVITY 58

WHO AM I?

The following biographical sketches are written in the first person. Read each sketch to your students and have them guess each person's name.

58-1 _____ Alexander Graham Bell _____

As a young man, I dedicated my life to teaching people who are hearing impaired. In my efforts to understand the causes of deafness, I studied sound vibrations and the human ear to learn how sound is transmitted through air. In my studies, I became greatly interested in the idea of being able to transmit speech over electrical wires. I knew it was possible, I just didn't know how.

My assistant, Thomas Watson, and I spent long hours, experimenting with this idea. One of the most exciting days of my life was March 10, 1876, just three days after my twenty-ninth birthday. I was sitting by a transmitter in one room and Watson was sitting with his ear next to a receiver in another room. I accidentally spilled some acid on my clothes and without thinking said, "Mr. Watson, come here, I want you."

Watson came running in from the other room shouting "I heard you." Surprised, I looked up and asked him what it was he heard. Excitedly, he responded, "You said, 'Watson come here.'" Suddenly, I realized that our experimental transmitter had worked. For the next several years, the telephone occupied most of my time, but I did not ignore my teaching. Even while Watson and I were perfecting our invention, I was busy organizing schools for children who are hearing impaired in different cities around the country.

I continued to work with people who were hearing impaired and to invent throughout my long life. While Thomas Edison made some improvements in the telephone I invented, I had the happy opportunity to improve upon the phonograph that he invented. Who am I?

Hindsight Questions
- What did Alexander Graham Bell invent?
- What else did he do with his life?

Insight Questions
- Why did Alexander Graham Bell do the things he did?
- What right did Bell have to do the things he did?

Foresight Questions
- How do you think Bell was rewarded for his choices?

Discussion Opportunity: Alexander Graham Bell was interested in making the world a better place in which to live. He took an interest in the needs of people with hearing problems and was gifted as an inventor, which enabled him to invent many useful things. It may be said he had a duty to use his talents to make the world a better place. His talents gave him the ability to do many things and he definitely had a right to do them as they harmed no one and helped many. He was willing to answer for his choices and was rewarded by a satisfying and happy life. Character Traits: PR right, RO caring, citizenship

---

58-2 .... Jessie James ....

I was born in the same year as Alexander Graham Bell, 1847, but my life was very different from his. Before I was sixteen, I had earned a reputation for being a good shot and for my daring. I was one of Quantrill's guerrillas fighting for the South during the Civil War. I liked the excitement of fighting. It was easier than working, and more profitable. So in 1866, after the war, my brother Frank and I formed a band of outlaws. I led the gang and planned our jobs.

Our first job was the bank at Liberty, Missouri. We made away with $58,000. Unfortunately, during the robbery, one of my men shot and killed George Wymore, a young college student. He and another student were walking by at the time of the robbery. My father had founded the William and Jewell college that Wymore attended in Liberty. I was sorry he had been killed, but in bank robberies, things like that happen.

For nearly sixteen years we terrorized people throughout the Midwest, robbing banks, trains, and stage coaches from Mexico to Minnesota. One of our most famous jobs was our attempt to rob the bank in Northfield, Minnesota. It was on September 7, 1876, just two days after I turned twenty-nine. This job went sour from the beginning. Some of the townspeople saw that the bank was being robbed and before it was over, three of my men were dead along with a bank clerk named Joseph Heywood. Frank was angry with Heywood because he wouldn't open the safe for us, so he shot him. The three Younger brothers were all wounded. We split up and they were captured two days later. Frank and I got away, but empty handed.

For the next eight years, I continued my profession. Sometimes Frank was with me and sometimes others. It was never hard to find someone interested in easy money.

I guess we did kill a lot of people along the way, but I don't really know how many. It wasn't something I kept track of. In order to get people to turn over their valuables to us, they had to know our guns were loaded and that we were willing to use them. Unfortunately, several innocent people were killed. That was just the nature of my work. In the end, I only lived to be thirty-five. Bob Ford, a member of my own gang, shot me in the back. Who am I?

Hindsight Questions
* What was Jessie James famous for?
* What else did he do with his life?

Insight Questions
* Why do you think Jesse James did the things he did?
* What right did James have to do the things he did?

Foresight Questions
* How was Jesse James rewarded for his choices?

Discussion Opportunity: Jesse James was greatly influenced by the Stink'n Think'n Gang. Iwannit Now, Li Fib, Biggs Bigger, and Eency Weency Tiny Too were his constant companions. He cared little for the rights of others and, when it was to his advantage, he took their property and sometimes their lives. He had the ability, but not the right to steal and kill. Eventually, he was held answerable for his choices by a bullet in the back.

It is interesting to compare his life with Alexander Graham Bell. They were born in the same year and 1876 was a big year for both of them. Bell invented the telephone and James attempted to rob a bank in Northfield. Two men who lived at the same time, but made very different choices. Character Traits: right, accountability; RO caring, citizenship; T honesty

ACTIVITY 59

I HAVE LONG OBSERVED ONE RULE

Read the following quotes from Benjamin Franklin to your students. After each ask them, either in writing or verbally, to tell you what they mean.

1. Franklin arrived in France on December 3, 1776. He was seventy years old and was one of three representatives from America.. Their mission was to encourage the French to side with America against England during the Revolutionary War. Shortly after arriving, Franklin received a letter from Juliana Rich warning him that his valet was probably a spy for the French government. Below is part of Franklin's reply to Mrs. Rich written on January 19, 1777, from Paris.

   "I have long observed one rule. It is simply this—to be concerned in no affairs that I would blush to have made public."

2. In 1732, at the age of twenty-six, Franklin thought of writing a book. He planned to call it *The Art of Virtue*. In his autobiography, he used this statement to describe a message he wanted to share with young people in that book.

   "Vicious acts are not hurtful because they are forbidden, but forbidden because they are hurtful."

3. Shortly after the treaty of Peace had been signed with great Britain, Franklin received a letter from John Jay. In his letter to Franklin, Jay commented that Franklin now had some enemies in England. This is part of Franklin's response to Jay, written from Passy, France, on January 6, 1784.

   "I have as you observe, some enemies in England, but they are my enemies as an American; I also have two or three in America, who are my enemies as a minister; but I thank God there are not in the whole world any who are my enemies as a man; for by His grace, through a long life, I have been enabled so to conduct myself that there does not exist a human being who can justly say, 'Ben Franklin has wronged me.' This my friend, is in old age a comfortable reflection."

Explain that taking ownership for our choices means we are willing to answer for those choices to others, to nature, and to ourselves. After discussing each quote ask:

• Is this quote talking about being answerable to others, to nature, or to ourselves?

Discussion Opportunity: A person with a clear conscience seldom has reason to fear the consequences of his or her choices and is willing to be answerable for them. We are answerable for our choices in three ways—we are answerable to others, to nature, and and to ourselves. If we offend others, they will try to make us pay. If we offend nature, we will be repaid by natural consequences. And our conscience will reprove us for bad intentions. Character Traits: PR ownership; T dependability

---

CHOOSING TO RESPECT MYSELF

Section Four

‿

LEARNING OBJECTIVES FOR SECTION FOUR

Recognize the Importance of Having Self-Respect

Identify Four Areas of Conduct that Will Create Self-Respect

    Self-Understanding

    Self-Denial

    Self-Reliance

    Selflessness

Desire to Possess Self-Respect

SECTION OVERVIEW

Benjamin Franklin wrote, "There is no happiness but in a virtuous and self-approving conduct." In the same place, he also wrote, "What is without us has not the least connection with happiness only so far as the preservation of our lives and health depends upon it." Unfortunately, all too many look for self-respect in the approval of others, often by doing things they cannot approve of themselves. But in the nature of things; self-respect can only be found within and, only then, as the result of a virtuous and self-approving conduct.

Four general areas of conduct may be relied on to help produce self-respect. They are self-understanding, self-denial, self-reliance, and selflessness.

Self-Understanding

To fully achieve your potential, it is important to understand two things: your strengths and your weaknesses. Strengths are what you must build on, weaknesses are what you must build around. Nature has endowed each of us with unique talents and gifts, which when used for virtuous purposes can produce satisfactions not achievable in any other way. At the same time, each of us has weaknesses. If we understand our weaknesses, we can generally find ways to work around or overcome them. For example, Thomas Edison was not good at math. For an inventor, this could be a serious shortcoming. His solution? Hire people who were good at math to work for him. Frederick Douglass didn't know how to read or write. His solution? Enlist other children to teach him.

Self-Denial

We all want things that would not be good for us if we got them. It is nearly impossible to do something you know is not good for you and still have self-respect. Indulging in harmful activities and substances creates feelings of weakness and guilt while denying oneself these things creates feelings of strength and freedom.

Self-Reliance

An important source of self-respect is the ability to rely on one's self. To do this requires the exercise of initiative and industriousness. It also requires a measure of independence, persistence, and patience in performing tasks and pursuing goals.

Selflessness

It has been said the best way to find oneself is in the service of others. This is because there is more of you to find. Few things can build self-respect better than doing good to others.

ACTIVITY 60

LANGUAGE OF SELF-RESPECT
Chalk Talk

How to Earn Self-Respect

Develop Self-Understanding
Get to know your interests, talents, abilities. Build on them.
Get to know your weaknesses and things you're not good at. Find workarounds.

Develop Self-Denial
Avoid harmful activities and substances, no matter how appealing
Avoid expressing anger and frustration in hurtful ways

Develop Self-Reliance
Take initiative
Be industrious and resourceful
Be patient and persistent
Be able to trust yourself

Develop Selflessness
Care about others, what they think, how they feel, what they need
Find ways to encourage, help, and uplift those around you

These are things we can do to develop self-resect. Those who do them find they like themselves better. They feel good about who they are and what they're doing.

Qualities of Self-Reliance

Initiative   Looks to see what needs to be done and does it, doesn't have to be told what to do

Independence   Works on own. Doesn't need a lot of guidance. Doesn't fool around when things need to be done.

Industriousness   Busy, active, hardworking, not lazy

Resourcefulness   Finds ways to solve problems

Resoluteness   Doesn't give up easy. Is persistent, patient, and determined

---

ACTIVITY 61

THE LITTLE APPLE SEED

61-1 _____ The Little Apple Seed Poem

ADVANCE PREPARATION: *Bring an apple and a knife to class.*

Show the apple to your class. Ask them to guess how many seeds are in the apple. Write their guesses on the board. Then cut the apple open and count the seeds. See which numbers were closest.

Show your students one of the seeds and ask them to guess how many apples are in that seed. Explain that if that seed were to be properly planted in the ground and taken care of, it would grow into a tree that would produce many apples a year for many years. Point out that each of those apples would also have seeds inside of them. Hold up an apple seed and ask if anyone can see a tree inside.

Read "The Little Apple Seed" poem on page 104.

Hindsight Questions
*   What grew from one little apple seed?
*   What did that apple tree do for people?

Insight Questions
*   How are you like this little apple seed?

Foresight Questions
*   What does the phrase ". . .wonderful and marvelous things from little seeds may grow." mean?

> **Discussion Opportunity:** Every child is born with the potential to do many interesting and worthwhile things. But like an apple seed, what we can become is not always obvious when we are little. As we discover our talents and learn to use them in ways that will help make the world a better place, we become like the apple tree bearing fruit. Character Traits: SR self-understanding

61-2 _____ The Little Apple Seed Activity Sheet

ADVANCE PREPARATION: *Photocopy page 105 for each student. Scissors and glue are also needed. Have them bring to school a baby picture, a current picture and one at an age in between. If they do not have pictures that can be glued to the sheet, make copies they can cut out and glue on the sheet.*

Give each student a copy of the "The _____ Seed" page and ask them to write their own name on the underlined space between "The" and "Seed." Have them glue pictures of themselves at different ages in the appropriate places. Let them write in their age at the time the picture was taken and write down things they were able to do at that age. The objective is to help them realize the growth they have already made and recognize they are in the process of developing their own potential to do many interesting and good things.

THE LITTLE APPLE SEED

by George L. Rogers

I'm so little now,
It's really hard to see,
All the full potential,
That's stored inside of me.

But when I'm fully grown,
It's not a seed you'll see,
But leaves, and fruit, and branches,
Upon an apple tree.

And an apple tree, after all,
Is quite a wondrous thing.
Each year, my pretty flowers
Will tell you when it's spring.

Birds will rest upon my limbs,
While children play below,
And each day through the summer,
My precious fruit will grow.

Then in the fall of every year,
When growing time is through,
I'll drop my apples on the ground,
And give them all to you.

To make apple pies and applesauce
Apple juice and cake.
Apple candy, apple tarts,
Apples raw and baked.

And as you eat these wondrous things,
You may wonder how indeed,
Came all these many apples
From such a little seed.

Now if you ask, how this can be?
It's a mystery I can't explain,
But this I know, my little friend,
With you it's much the same.

Like me, you are little yet,
And so it's hard to see,
And know the full potential
Of all that you can be.

But each time you eat an apple,
Just remember what you know,
That wonderful and marvelous things,
From little seeds may grow.

The _____ Seed

This is me when I was _____ old. When I was this age I

_____

_____

PICTURE

_____

_____

_____

This is me when I was _____ old. When I was this age I

_____

_____

PICTURE

_____

_____

_____

This is me now. At this age I _____

_____

_____

PICTURE

_____

_____

_____

ACTIVITY 62

DISCOVERING MY TALENTS AND INTERESTS

62-1 _____ In the News _____

ADVANCE PREPARATION: Photocopy page 108 for each student who will be conducting an interview. *Invite older students to interview members of your class using the interview form. Alternatively, class members may interview each other. If possible, have a camera available for them to take a picture of the student they interviewed.*

For the next several days, read to the class the answers to the questions for one or more of the students and have the rest of the class guess who the student is. Alternatively, place the interview sheets on the wall under the heading "In the News" for everyone to see.

Explore with your students the idea that who they are now is not who they will eventually become. Point out that, if they make the effort, they will continually discover new and exciting things about themselves throughout their lives. Their interests will change, their abilities will increase, and they will have larger capacities for doing useful and worthwhile things.

62-2 _____ I Write My Own Story _____

Several days prior to class, ask your students to pretend they are now sixty years old and looking back on their lives. From this perspective, assign them to write a one- or two-page autobiography. The autobiography is to include things they have actually done so far in life and things they think they would like to do over the next fifty years. In class, have them share what they wrote. Then ask and discuss:

1) What did you learn about yourself from this activity?
2) How do each of us write our own stories every day?

Point out that by choosing what we do and how we use our time we not only write our story for today, but also lay the foundation from which we work in the future. Help them to see each day as a blank page on which they can write something worthwhile, but they have to make the effort.

Discussion Opportunity: One of the most important things you can do is to discover what your talents are and how to use them in ways that are helpful to yourself and others. Iwannit Now may try to make you impatient. Eency Weency Tiny Too may try to make you think your talents are unimportant or that you are not as good as others. But, just as apple seeds do not become trees overnight, neither will you become all that you can become overnight. However, the more you rely on the skills of Criticism, Curiosity, Concentration and Correction, the greater will be your self-understanding and the less influence the Stink'n think'n Gang can have on you. Character Traits: RO self-understanding

---

62-3 ———————————— What Am I Doing? ————————————

ADVANCE PREPARATION: *Photocopy the activity sheet on page 109 for each student.*
Have students complete the activity sheet.

Hindsight Questions
* Which of these activities can you do?
* Which of these activities most affect your future?

Insight Questions
* How can recognizing what you are good at help you understand yourself better?
* What is required of a person to learn to read, write, ride a bicycle, and play a piano?

Foresight Questions
* Why is it important to learn new skills?
* Why is it important to get help when you are having difficulty learning a necessary skill?

62-4 ———————— Discovering My Strengths and Weaknesses ————————

ADVANCE PREPARATION: *Photocopy page 110 for each student. Discuss the HIF questions below.*

62-5 ———————————— I Have a Talent ————————————

ADVANCE PREPARATION: *Photocopy page 111 for each student. Discuss the HIF questions below.*

Hindsight Questions
* What did you learn from completing this activity sheet? (110 or 111)

Insight Questions
* Why may things you like to do be considered strengths?
* Why is it important to understand your strengths and weaknesses?
* How can discovering your talents make life more fun?

Foresight Questions
* How is it possible to turn weaknesses into strengths?
* Why is it important to develop your talents?

> **Discussion Opportunity:** Learning new skills helps us gain self-respect. Each skill may be useful and beneficial. Each new skill increases our ability to do things. But learning new skills requires the use of our thinking skills, especially Communication, Concentration, and Correction. In addition learning new skills requires a high degree of self-reliance including the qualities of initiative, industriousness, persistence, and patience. Character Traits: SR self-reliance

IN THE NEWS
Interview Sheet

NAME: _____

BIRTH DATE: _____

WHERE BORN: _____

_____

photograph

FAVORITE FOOD: _____

FAVORITE GAME : _____

FAVORITE TOY: _____

FAVORITE TV SHOW: _____

FAVORITE THING TO DO: _____

NEXT YEAR I WANT TO: _____

I WANT TO LEARN HOW TO: _____

WHEN I GROW UP I WANT TO: _____

_____

What Am I Doing?

Draw a line from the riddle to the drawing of the activity it describes.

My feet determine fast or slow,
My hands select which way to go,
And perched upon my seat so high,
I see the ground beneath me fly.

Images form upon my brain,
Of colors and sounds so very plain,
Of people and places beyond my sight,
But all I see is black and white.

My left hand does one thing,
My right hand something other,
My left foot does something else,
And my right foot still another.

Yet no one seems to mind,
As they give a listening ear,
For they care not what they see,
But only what they hear.

As my hand moves up and down,
In movements straight and movements
   round,
With shapes of one and twenty-five
My very thoughts all come alive.

DISCOVERING MY STRENGTHS AND WEAKNESSES

I learned that I really liked to _____

when I _____

_____

_____

_____

I tried to _____ but found I did not enjoy it

because _____

_____

_____

_____

I would really like to _____ because it would help

me _____

_____

_____

_____

It was really hard for me to _____, but I'm glad

I did because _____

_____

_____

I HAVE A TALENT

1. A special talent, interest, or ability I have is:

    _____

2. The way I discovered my interest was:

    _____

    _____

    _____

3. Some things I am doing to develop this talent or interest are:

    _____

    _____

    _____

4. Some ways I would like to use this talent, interest, or ability in the future are:

    _____

    _____

    _____

5. This talent, interest, or ability is important to me because:

    _____

    _____

    _____

BIOGRAPHY

BEATRIX UNDERSTANDS

Once upon a time, there was a little girl named Beatrix Potter. She lived in a large house with nine servants, but Beatrix was very lonely.

Her parents were not much interested in Beatrix. She lived in a room on the third floor which she only left when she was invited. Her parents lived in another part of the house and rarely came to see her. Beatrix was taken care of by McKenzie, her nurse. McKenzie brought her meals to her, but Beatrix ate alone. McKenzie took Beatrix for walks each day, but seldom had much to say.

Apart from her daily walks, the only view Beatrix had of the outside world was through a barred window in her room. From there she could look down on the street and watch people pass by in their fine clothes and elegant coaches.

Sometimes, Beatrix's grandmother would read or tell her stories. One day, when she was six years old, her grandmother wanted to tell her about the Cromptons. Her grandmother said, "I was a Crompton before I married your grandfather. The Cromptons were people who did things. They were people who knew how to work."

Just then, they heard footsteps. It was Beatrix's father. Almost instinctively, Beatrix slid under the table so her father wouldn't see her. Her grandmother patted her reassuringly on the top of her head and then Beatrix heard a conversation that gave her the courage to eventually reach out and do things that would someday make her famous.

Grandmother Potter told Beatrix's father she was worried about him and his family. He had been born into wealth and had now become idle, doing nothing of importance with either his intelligence or his abilities. She told him that she wanted her grandchildren to live life. She didn't want them to just be blotters to absorb it. She wanted them to do something with their lives, not just exist. She reminded him of his Crompton heritage, that they were workers, people of character and conscience. Beatrix listened in wonder to a story about Samuel Crompton, who invented a new kind of spinning wheel, and to tales of other Cromptons.

Sitting underneath the table, Beatrix understood what her grandmother was trying to tell her. She recognized that if she was determined enough, she would not always have to live behind bars.

But it was also scary. Though she was lonely, she felt safe in her third-floor room. To actually run and play with other children was frightening. What would they think of a girl who didn't know how to do those things? Would they think she was stupid or laugh at her? Would they even notice her?

Hindsight Questions
- What was Beatrix's childhood like?
- What was Beatrix's grandmother telling her?

Insight Questions
- Why was Beatrix frightened?

Foresight Questions
- What are some risks in trying to do new things?

Discussion Opportunity: Although Beatrix had an unhappy childhood, she understood that if she wanted to make something of her life, it was up to her. Biggs Bigger tried to frighten her by making her afraid of what others would think of her. Eency Weency Tiny Too tried to make her feel little. But the Seven C Skills came to her aid. Criticism gave her understanding and Control helped her overcome her fears. Communication and Creativity helped discover her talents and she became a famous children's writer. She wrote 33 children's books of which Peter Rabbit was her most famous. Character Traits: SR self-understanding, self-reliance

BIOGRAPHY

ACTIVITY 64

LOUISA'S PLUMMY CAKE

Louisa Allcott, the author of *The Little House on the Prairie* books, records this experience from her childhood.

"Another memory is of my fourth birthday, which was celebrated at my father's schoolroom in the Masonic Temple in Boston. All the children were there. I wore a crown of flowers, and stood on a table to give out cakes to each child as the procession marched past. By some oversight the cakes fell short, and I saw that if I gave away the last one I should have none. As I was queen of the party, I felt I ought to have it. I held on to it tightly till my mother said, 'It is always better to give away than to keep nice things, so I know my Louy will not let the little friend go without.'

"The little friend received that dear plummy cake, and I a kiss and my first lesson in the sweetness of self-denial, a lesson which my mother beautifully illustrated all her long life."

Hindsight Questions
- What did Louisa give up to please her mother and to make her friend happy?

Insight Questions
- How did giving the plummy cake to her friend make Louisa feel good about herself?
- What is the sweetness in self-denial Louisa is talking about?
- How can self-denial and selflessness make a person happy?

Foresight Questions
- What lesson did Louisa learn?
- What was the advantage of learning that lesson early in life?

Discussion Opportunity: Louisa might have had some temporary pleasure in eating the cake and not giving it to her guest, but the reflection of having given it up to her guest gave her a sense of satisfaction for many years. Iwannit Now will try to convince you that immediate pleasure is what you want, but pleasures of sense, by their very nature, are temporary and can never give lasting satisfaction. Self-denial, on the other hand gives a person inner strength and selflessness allows a person to be generous, kind and helpful to others. These qualities bring the satisfaction of having done something useful and give a person peace of mind. Character Traits: SR self-denial, selflessness; RO Caring

ACTIVITY 65

MAC AND ZACH AND THE RUSTY HORSESHOE

by George L. Rogers
Illustrations by Stefanie Eskander

One day near old Hackensack Track
Some boys were playing with Mac and Zach Black,
When one of them found an old rusty horseshoe,
And hollered, "Hey guys, here's something to do!
Let's see who's best, who's better than who,
By who can throw farther this rusty horseshoe!"

Mac threw it far with a mighty fine fling,
And it sailed through the air with plenty of zing.
But when Tommy threw farther that rusty horseshoe,
And said to Mac, "Guess who's better than who?"
Mac became angry, and really quite mad,
And called Tommy some names that were really quite bad.

Mac pouted and shouted. He ranted and raved.
The game wasn't fair the way Tommy had played.
Tommy had cheated in the way that he threw,
And that's how he threw farther that rusty horseshoe.

The two boys looked at each other, then bristled and bustled,
They quibbled and quarreled, and eventually they tussled.
You're either winner or loser, that's how they thought,
And to prove who was better, that's the reason they fought.

But when they were finished and the battle was done,
And each one was claiming, he was the one who had won,
The other boys looked at them and tried hard to guess,
Whether it was Tommy or Mac that was more of a mess.

On their way home, Zach said to Mac his twin brother,
"I wish when we were playing, that somehow or other,
We could just play and have lots of fun,
Without worrying so much over who lost or who won.

"Sure it's nice to be the one in first place,
But isn't it good just to be in the race?
And after the contest, aren't there things to be done,
That have nothing to do with who lost or who won?"

But Mac was caught up in the thick of thin things,
He disliked the thinking such questioning brings.
So he said to Zach, "Don't be such a nerd.
What you are saying is truly absurd."

"You know that people like best other people who win.
So if you want to be popular, and if you want to be in,
You've got to be first, at the front of the pack."
And that's how he thought, the brother of Zach.

Then Mac furrowed his brow in sort of a pout,
For deep down inside he was beginning to doubt,
"Isn't it true what I've always thought,
That happiness comes and is easily bought?

"Isn't it looks and designer clothes,
Physical strength and what one knows,
Talent and ability, charm and wit,
Aren't these the things that make one it?"

"But if it's being first ahead of the rest,
And being on top that makes one best,
Why am I not happier than my brother Zach?
What does he have that I still lack?"

Now tell me quick in voices low,
From what you've heard and what you know,
What's the difference between Mac and Zach?
And if you can tell me what Mac may lack,
I'd like you to do so, and I'd like you to now.
Please give me the whatfor, the whyfor, and how.

Hindsight Questions
- Why did Tommy and Mac fight?
- Who came out the winner?

Insight Questions
- What is wrong with "Who's better than who" thinking?
- What was Mac's belief about what it took to be happy?
- How happy was he when he and Tommy were fighting?
- What was Mac beginning to question?

Foresight Questions
- How can self-control help make a person happier with himself or herself?

Discussion Opportunity: Iwannit Now tries to convinces you that happiness is obtained by having certain things and by being popular. Biggs Bigger wants you to think that having more of these things than someone else will makes you better than them. Eency Weency Tiny Too wants you to think that, indeed others are less important. Criticism and Curiosity are trying to help Mac see things differently, but he is resisting their influence. Zach, on the other hand, has things figured out. Character Traits: SR self-denial; RO citizenship

BIOGRAPHY

THE SCHOOL THAT MARY BUILT

Mary tried hard to hold back the tears. She was very hurt, but didn't want to show it. It was true, she couldn't read, but why was the girl so angry at her just for picking up the book. Why did she lash out so harshly, "Put that book down, you can't read." Mary quietly put the book down. But, from that moment on, Mary felt that learning to read was one of the most important things she could ever do.

Mary was the first free-born child of Samuel and Patsy McLeod. She was born July 10, 1875 in Maysville, South Carolina. Her older brothers and sisters had been born as slaves and later sold as slaves. After becoming free, her father and mother, through much hard work had purchased a small amount of land on which they grew cotton. From the time she was a little child, Mary picked cotton on her father's farm. Her family was better off than many. Most of their neighbors were poor sharecroppers, farmers who farmed land owned by others in return for a share of the crop.

One day, a Miss Emma Wilson came to visit the family. She was starting a school for black children. Mary's parents had several school-age children, but they were needed in the cotton field. Their livelihood depended on it. But recognizing Mary's strong desire to learn, and thinking that, with a little extra effort they could spare one set of hands, her parents made an important decision. Mary could attend the school.

The school itself was just a shack with few supplies, but Mary thrived and quickly learned to read and write. During her second year of school, Mary was introduced to numbers. She decided numbers were as wonderful and useful as words. As her ability to read and understand numbers increased, she became aware of how many uneducated small farmers and sharecroppers like her father were kept poor because they were being cheated.

Mary received a personal lesson when one day she went with her father to sell his cotton. She noticed that the man buying the cotton told the man in front of them that his cotton weighed four hundred pounds. But Mary could see that the scale said five hundred pounds. So, before the man could say anything when he put her father's cotton on the scale, Mary spoke out, "Oh look, father, we've got six hundred pounds of cotton." For the first time, Samuel was paid full price for his cotton and made a small profit. Soon, neighbors were coming to Mary to ask for her help in figuring their bills and writing letters. These experiences convinced Mary how important it is for people to be able to read and write and to understand the use of numbers.

When Mary had completed Miss Wilson's school, she was able to continue her education at Scotia Seminary in Concord, North Carolina. Her family did not have the money to send her, but Mary received a scholarship provided by Mary Crissman, a seamstress in Denver, Colorado who offered her life savings as a scholarship so that one black child could get an education. With this assistance, twelve-year old Mary entered Scotia Seminary in 1887. Later Mary was to say of Mary Crissman's gift, "To this day, my heart thrills with gratitude at the memory of that day. I was but a little girl, groping for the light, ...and away off in Denver, Colorado, a poor dressmaker, sewing for her daily bread, heard my call and came to my assistance. Out of her scanty earnings she invested in a life....my life!"

After graduating, Mary returned to Mayfield to teach. But Mary had a dream of one day building a school of her own. That opportunity came in 1903. Mary heard that in Daytona, Florida, blacks were being hired to lay tracks for the Florida East Coast Railroad. There were no schools for black children in Daytona and living conditions for families of the workers were awful. Children were being reared in conditions of filth, poverty, and ignorance.

With $1.50 in her purse, Mary Bethune, her husband, Burt, and their son left for Daytona. Immediately after arriving she made plans to start a school. Mary found a small cottage she could rent for $11 a month. It was dirty and needed repair, but it had possibilities. Mary got busy, and within a few days her school began with five students. Mary charged a tuition of fifty cents a week. It was not enough to cover the costs, but it was all she felt the children could afford to pay. She had to learn to be a fund raiser. Mary discovered that there were many people in Daytona who were willing to help, and with donations of ten cents, twenty-five cents, one dollar, or sometimes as much as five dollars, her school began to slowly move forward. At first students used charcoal for pencils and boiled berries for ink. Her desk was an old packing box. During the first year it was common for neighbors to see her rummaging through trash heaps for things that could be reused. She and her students baked sweet potato pies to raise money.

By 1905 Mary's school had one hundred students. They desperately needed a bigger building. But Mary didn't have any land to build on and no money to build with. Undaunted, she found a trash dump the owner was willing to sell for $250. This would be the land they would build on. Mary committed to buy the dump site and within a week had the $15 necessary for down payment. She gave it to the owner in pennies, nickels, and dimes wrapped in a handkerchief.

Mary's school emphasized a sound academic education but also provided the girls with home-making skills such as cooking and sewing. Mary believed there was no such thing as menial labor, only menial self-esteem. She taught her students the importance of cleanliness for which she received the title of "dirt chaser." Daily cleaning and personal hygiene were requirements for attending her school. Her students also called her "Mother Dear" because of their closeness to her.

Eventually her school became the Bethune-Cookman College and still stands today, nearly a hundred years later. During those many years, thousands of young people have received the education they needed to live successful and fulfilling lives. All thanks to the school that Mary built.

Hindsight Questions
- Why did Mary feel it was so important to get an education?
- What did she discover about numbers?
- What opportunities did the ability to read and count make possible for Mary?

Insight Questions
- Which of the Seven C Skills did Mary have to use to get an education?
- Which incidents in Mary's life show she was a self-starter?
- Why was Mary able to accomplish so much with so little?

Foresight Questions
- Which qualities did Mary have that you would most like to have?

Discussion Opportunity: Mary's life demonstrates several qualities that are necessary to self-respect. She was able to discover talents and interests that enabled her to live a productive and useful life. She was a self-starter who was able to find out how to get things done. She was very caring and dedicated her life to doing good things for others. Character Traits: SR self-reliance; RO caring, citizenship

ACTIVITY 67

THE DOCTOR OF LAMBARÉNÉ

"But that chicken coop is filthy. Haven't you seen it?" he exclaimed.

"Yes," she replied, "but it is the only unused building on the island, and we don't have time to build anything else. You said yourself, you could not continue to examine and treat these poor souls out in the open as you did yesterday."

The doctor listened as the nurse, his wife, Helene, suggested that they put lime on the floors, fill in the holes in the roof, and whitewash the walls. They could build some shelves for the medicine and put a bed in there for patients to lie on when he was treating them. It might not be great, but it would be better than what they had.

They had only been on the island for a few hours before a whole fleet of canoes, loaded with the sick and dying, had begun arriving. In this remote part of the Congo, also known as French Equatorial Africa, there had not been a medical doctor for many years. In fact, it was a missionary pamphlet pleading for a doctor to come to this region that had led Albert Schweitzer to give up his promising career as rector of the Theological School of Strasbourg University and as an accomplished organist, to study medicine. It had taken him over eight years to prepare for this very moment. And yet how unprepared he felt. He was so grateful Helene had spent those years preparing to be a nurse so she could help him.

Albert agreed it could work, and after all, they didn't really have any other options. Outside were dozens of people who were so ill it was a serious question as to how many of them could even be saved. Enlisting all the help they could get, Albert and Helene set to work, feverishly cleaning and getting the chicken coop ready to serve as the first hospital in Lambaréné. In short order they were in a position to give serious attention to their patients.

At first, they tried to separate the urgent from the less urgent cases. But all were urgent. In every case it was a race against death. Some they lost. But over the days and weeks, a great many recovered. Progress was made. Weeks turned into months. Months turned into years. Eventually, little by little, they cleared away the jungle, built more buildings, and the hospital at Lambaréné expanded. To be sure, there were many setbacks—epidemics, two world wars, and elephants tearing up the gardens, but through it all, natives received critical medical treatment that had been denied them before the Schweitzers had come.

In time, other doctors joined them, and many good-hearted people from around the world donated medical supplies and other critical items that went into building the hospital. It was the money Albert received for the Nobel Peace Prize in 1952 that enabled him to build the compound for patients with leprosy. Treatment was even given to sick animals, both wild and domestic. Many stayed and became part of the little village that now made up Lambaréné.

Albert's reverence for life might well be summed up by his statement to an interviewer: "What the world needs most is [people] who occupy themselves with the needs of other [people]. In this unselfish labor a blessing falls on both the helper and the helped. . . .As soon as we open our eyes and deliberately search, we see many who need help—not in big things, but in the littlest things. Wherever a man turns he can find someone who needs him."

Hindsight Questions
- What did Albert Schweitzer feel the world needs most?

Insight Questions
- How did the Albert and Helene demonstrate the qualities of self-reliance?
- What other qualities of self-respect did they possess?

Foresight Questions
- Why could the Schweitzers feel good about what they had done?

Discussion Opportunity: Albert and Helene Schweitzer weren't people to sit around and complain about their problems. They realized there are many whose needs are much greater and that everyone has someone who needs them, if they are willing to give of themselves. Creativity and self-reliance were among the many skills the Schweitzers developed in their efforts to serve others. In going to Africa, they denied themselves many comforts they might have had, but they gained far more in the love, friendships, and experiences they had in Lambaréné. Character Traits: SR selflessness, self-denial

---

BIOGRAPHY

ACTIVITY 68

JANE'S DECLARATION

"I recall an incident which must have occurred before I was seven years old, for the mill in which my father transacted his business that day was closed in 1867. The mill stood in the neighboring town adjacent to its poorest quarter.

"Before then I had always seen the little city of ten thousand people with the admiring eyes of a country child, and it had never occurred to me that all its streets were not as attractive as the one which contained the glittering toy shop and the confectioner.

"On that day, I had my first sight of real poverty with all its suffering, and felt the curious difference between country poverty and city poverty with its dark, shabby, dirty streets.

"I remember asking my father why people lived in such horrid little houses so close together, and that after receiving his explanation I declared with much firmness that when I grew up I should, of course, have a large house, but it would not be built among the other large houses, but right in the midst of the horrid little houses like these."

Jane Addams went on to found Hull House in Chicago, the first and most famous settlement house for people living in slum conditions. For her work with the poor and her work with the International League for Peace and Freedom, she was a co-winner of the 1931 Nobel Peace Prize.

Hindsight Questions
- How old was Jane when she decided she wanted to help people who were living in poverty?

Insight Questions
- How did Jane demonstrate the qualities of self-reliance?

Foresight Questions
- What is there about helping others that can make people feel good about themselves?

ACTIVITY 69

WHAT SHOULD REUBEN DO?

The game was done
It had been fun
But now that they were through

She left it there
Upon the chair
And then his sister Sue

Said put it back
Upon the rack
I leave it up to you

To put away
The game this day
What should Reuben do?

He wants to play
On this nice day
Before his chores are through

The sun is bright
His heart is light
His friends all say, "Let's do."

We'll play some ball
Behind that wall
And you'll be out of view

But should he shirk
And leave his work
What should Reuben do?

He was not glad
And got quite mad
When Tyler took his shoe

And by the string
Gave it a fling
And in the air it threw

But then when Kim
Made fun of him
And then she said P U

He felt real bad
And was quite sad
What should Reuben do?

It gave him fright
To see the sight
Of everyone he knew

To say a poem
In front of them
Seemed more than he could do

He felt quite weak
And couldn't speak
He turned a reddish hue

So feeling queer
With all that fear
What should Reuben do?

Discussion Opportunity: Reuben has to make several choices, all of which affect how he will feel about himself. Iwannit Now, along with Biggs Bigger and Eency Weency Tiny Too are all working on him, but if he has developed his C skills, he can call on Criticism and Control to help him out of these problems. If he gives in to anger or fear, he will think less of himself. The same is true if he leaves his work and fails to do his duty. Character Traits: SR self-denial

CHOOSING
TO
RESPECT OTHERS

Section Five

∾

LEARNING OBJECTIVES FOR SECTION FIVE

Appreciate three ways in which we show our respect for others

    Caring

    Fairness

    Honoring

Recognize that all people have common needs

Understand how individual differences help us meet common needs

SECTION OVERVIEW

The scriptural injunction, "Therefore all things whatsoever ye would that others should do to you, do ye even so to them" is by far the best guide to mutual respect ever given. Known as the Golden Rule, it has been endorsed by philosophers of all ages. But for all its merit, the Golden Rule is not the general rule, and as the words of a song remind us, "Hate is strong and mocks the song of Peace on Earth Good Will to Men."

There are many causes for the lack of mutual respect, but none that aren't related to personal choices people make. Some have to do with differences in religious, political, or philosophical beliefs. Some have to do with differences in racial or ethnic origin. Other causes of disrespect arise out of pure selfishness, unleashing the purple passions of greed and lust. Not infrequently, the inability to respect others arises from a lack of self-respect. Sometimes, simple misunderstandings unleash torrents of hate and revenge. But whatever the cause, when such feelings arise, the Golden Rule goes out the door and people do things to others they would never in a hundred years want to have done to themselves. Whether manifested in rudeness and incivility or in pogroms for exterminating ethnic minorities, lack of respect for others is a plague that robs the human family of both peace and prosperity.

Three important ways in which respect may be manifest are caring, fairness, and honoring.

Caring

When we truly care about others, we will more likely treat them respectfully. While it is far easier to care for others when we feel they care for us, becoming a caring person is something we can choose to do independently of what anyone else does.

Fairness

A commitment to play by the rules, to treat others impartially, and to be just in our relations with others is another way in which we manifest respect for others. Caring is a pre-requisite to fairness. Only caring people will choose to be fair in dealing with others.

Honoring

Honoring the personal and property rights of others is perhaps the highest manifestation of respect. Caring and Fairness are prerequisites to Honoring. Honoring is the basic objective of the U.S. Constitution and is the foundation on which civilization rests.

For children to grasp these ideas and be meaningful to them they must understand two fundamental things.
  1) That every living person has the same basic needs and in this respect we are all created equal, and
  2) That individual differences are essential to our mutual well-being, for it is these very differences that enable us to meet our common needs and that provide the interest and variety so necessary to life.

ACTIVITY 70

THE LANGUAGE OF RESPECT

70-1 _____ Chalk Talk _____

Write the words in the left column on the board. Randomly select definitions from the middle column and have your students tell you which word the definition matches. After writing all the definitions on the board, ask for specific examples of caring, loving, honoring, considerate, fair, kind, and courteous behaviors and note them in the right column.

CARING	To be interested in, concerned about, to watch over and look after	Taking care of a sick person, feeding a baby, helping a friend,
HONOR	A high regard for	Obeying laws and rules; taking care of your own property, taking care of the environment, not hurting others
CONSIDERATE	Mindful of others' needs and feelings	Sharing your toys, lunch, etc., Picking up your own mess, not interrupting others or making a disturbance
FAIRNESS	To be just, impartial, follow rules, and not take advantage of others	Don't cheat, don't take more than your share, don't prejudge others
KIND	To be gentle, good hearted	Shovel snow for elderly person, help cat out of tree, give money to needy person
COURTEOUS	To be well mannered, polite and civil	Say please, thank you, etc; let other persons go first, avoid rudeness

70-2 _____ Language of Respect Activity Sheet _____

ADVANCE PREPARATION: *Photocopy page 125 for students to complete.*

Discussion Opportunity: The words we use reflect the quality of our thoughts. Nameit Blameit and Judge B. Fore will encourage you to speak rudely and treat others roughly. But don't give in to them. Use your thinking skills to decide what kind of a person you really want to be. How you treat others says a whole lot more about you than it does about them. In addition, how you treat others has a lot to do with how others will treat you in return. Character Traits: RO caring, fairness, citizenship

LANGUAGE OF RESPECT

Draw a circle around the words or phrases you think are respectful things to say.

Thank You   I Hate You

Shut Up   May I

Stupid   Give Me That

Please   I'm Sorry

Idiot   You're Welcome

Is This a Respectful Thing to Say?

Write a yes in front of the statements you think are respectful things to say.

_____   Mother, may I go play with Tara?

_____   Thank you for helping me.

_____   Give me the potatoes.

_____   Get out of the way old man.

_____   Want to play? Go play with a monkey.

_____   Hello, Mrs. Aba, can I give you a hand?

ACTIVITY 71

INDIVIDUAL DIFFERENCES HELP MEET COMMON NEEDS

71-1 _____ Crayons, Colors, and People _____

ADVANCE PREPARATION: *Photocopy page 128 for each student.*
Have your students choose a crayon and color one picture on the sheet entirely with that crayon. Now allow them to use any colors they wish to use to color the other picture on the sheet.

Hindsight Questions
* How are your crayons alike? How are they different?

Insight Questions
* Which picture do you like best? Why?

Foresight Questions
* Which do you think is better, having many colors or having few colors to choose from?

Discussion Opportunity: Different colors not only add variety, beauty, and interest to life, but are necessary to help us tell things apart. The likeness between crayons give them a common purpose. Their differences make it easier for them to accomplish this purpose. The same is true with people. If there were only boys or only girls, there would never be any other people. If everyone were farmers, who would make shoes? If we were all the same size, shape, and color, who could tell us apart? The ability to recognize how our differences can make life better for all of us is the beginning of respect. Character Traits: RO caring, fairness, citizenship

---

71-2 _____ What if? _____

To illustrate how individual differences are essential to our mutual well-being, have your students select one of the "What If Activities" below and use it to explore one of the "What If Questions." The idea is to have them think about what life would be like if there were no differences between people and things.

What If Activities:
Tell a story
Write a paper
Create a play
Make a picture

What If Questions:
What if everyone was exactly like me?
What if there were only one kind of tree, animal, etc.?
What if every musician wanted to play the same instrument?
What if every person wanted to be a doctor, shoemaker, etc.?
What if the weather never changed?
What if there was only one letter in the alphabet?

71-3 The Pencil and the Paper

Read the following story starter about the pencil and the paper to your students. Either individually or in small groups, ask them to create a story or a skit about how the pencil and the paper discover how much they need each other to reach their full potential.

Said the pencil to the paper, "You're not at all like me.
And what you may be good for, I simply cannot see."
"Well!" said the paper. "You're surely not my kind.
I'll gladly go my way and leave you here behind.
You do what pencils do, whatever that may be.
The only thing I ask, is stay away from me."

Hindsight Questions
• What did the pencil and paper think of each other?

Insight Questions
• In what ways are a pencil and paper alike?
• How do their differences make them far more useful together than either of them could be alone?
• How are a pencil and paper like people who are different?

Foresight Questions
• In noticing differences between people, what is something good to look for?

71-4 Mother Nature Changes Her Mind

Read the following story to your students.
One day, Mother Nature said to herself, "Life would be so much easier if there were not so many different kinds of plants, insects, animals, birds, and fish. To simplify things from now on, I am going to only have one kind of plant, one kind of insect, one kind of animal, one kind of bird, and one kind of fish. But I'll need some help in deciding which kind of each to have.

There is a (your) grade class at (your) Elementary School that is really smart. I'll ask them to help me decide which kind of each that I should keep."

Divide your class into small groups to discuss which kind of plant, insect, animal, bird, and fish they would advise Mother Nature to keep. In deciding, they are to take into account the usefulness of each creature in supporting human life and what life would be like without those creatures. If they do not agree with Mother Nature's project, have them decide what they would say to make her change her mind.

Hindsight Questions
• How difficult is it to choose only one kind of each plant, insect, bird, and fish?

Insight Questions
• Why is it necessary to have a wide variety of animal and plant life?
• How do all these plants, insects, animals, birds, and fishes depend on each other for their existence?

Foresight Questions
• Why is it important to take care of and preserve variety in plant and animal life?

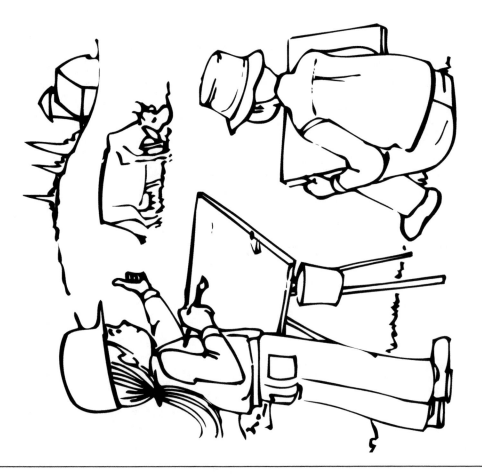

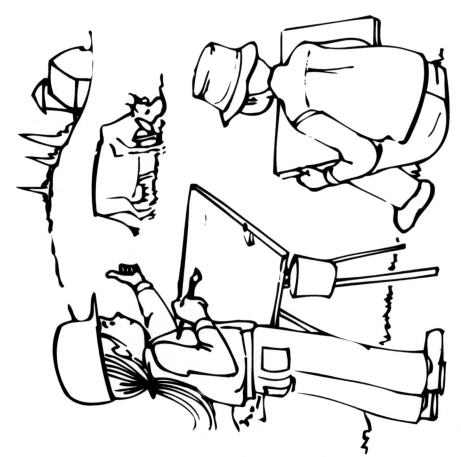

Four Things All People Need

To find four things all people need, write the first letter of the name of each object in the space below the object. For example, A for apple.

A   _____   _____

_____   _____   _____   _____

_____   _____   _____   _____

_____

ACTIVITY 72

ALL ARE EQUAL

Use one or more of the following activities to demonstrate ways in which all people are alike. After the activity, discuss how every living person has essentially the same need for food, water, rest, shelter, transportation, love, education, and opportunity. Explore how all people have thoughts and feelings, experience joy and sadness, and have talents and skills they can contribute to the mutual good. Point out that when we talk about "all men being created equal" in the Declaration of Independence, we are talking about the ways in which we are all alike. That is what being equal means.

72-1   Things All People Need Puzzle

ADVANCE PREPARATION: *Photocopy the activity sheet on page 129 for students. After completing the activity, discuss the following questions with them.*

Hindsight Questions
* Why are each of these considered needs?

Insight Questions
* In what way are all people created equal?
* What happens when individuals are denied these needs?
* What happens when people don't work together in helping each other meet these needs?

Foresight Questions
* What happens when we are careless with our own needs or those of others?
* How do these needs provide us opportunity and purpose?

> **Discussion Opportunity:** All people are created equal in that we have the same basic needs. Our differences help us in meeting these common needs. Some people know how to grow food. Some know how to build machines. Others know how to make clothing. Still others build houses, and so on. No one knows how to do everything and everyone knows how to do something. And in the world, there are always those who have serious needs that we may be able to help. Recognizing this can give purpose and direction to our lives. It can provide opportunities to use our talents in meaningful ways doing things that are important and worthwhile. The Stink'n Think'n Gang tells us to only care about our own wants and needs, not those of others. The Seven C's help us recognize that doesn't work because we all need each other. Character Traits: RO caring, fairness, citizenship

72-2   Likeness Pantomime

Select eight students. Have each act out one of the following activities. Have the rest of the class guess what each one is doing. The activities are: breathing, eating, sleeping, getting dressed, hugging, crying, laughing, and reading. Discuss the HIF questions below.

72-3   Likeness Art Project

With your students, brainstorm a list of as many ways in which all people are alike. Then give each student a colored piece of paper on which to draw a person doing one of these things. When the pictures are complete, make a patchwork quilt with them on one wall of your classroom. Discuss the HIF questions below.

72-4   Likeness Montage

Divide your class into small groups. Provide each group with newspapers and magazines from which to cut out pictures of people engaged in a variety of activities. Have them paste these pictures into a montage depicting ways in which all people are alike and then have each group present and explain their picture to the rest of the class. Discuss the HIF questions below.

Hindsight Questions
* In what ways are all people alike or equal?

Insight Questions
* How important is the idea of equality to the American way of life?
* What are some ways in which we can honor each others needs?
* What happens when when people do not honor each other's needs?

Foresight Questions
* Why is it important for you to honor the needs of others?
* How can helping others meet their needs give more purpose and meaning to your own life?

Discussion Opportunity: Equality is a simple concept, but many people have difficulty with it. It means all people have the same right to provide for the necessities of life, and the same right to pursue life, liberty, and happiness. The Stink'n Think'n Gang often succeeds in convincing people to pursue their own happiness at the expense of others. But, people who care about the Declaration of Independence and about other people will respect the property and rights of others, and will do what they can to help them meet their needs. Character Traits: RO caring, fairness, citizenship

---

ACTIVITY 73

EMPATHY ACTIVITIES

Most people have similar experiences when subjected to similar circumstances. To demonstrate, use one of the following empathy activities. Discuss the HIF questions below.

73-1 ———— Blindfolded Games ————

Play Pin the Tail on the Donkey, blindfolded.

Toss a ball or waded paper into a wastepaper basket, blindfolded

Walk from point "A" to point "B," blindfolded

73-2 ———— One Handed Activity ————

Have each student place their dominant hand behind their back and ask them to perform one of the following activities with their other hand. Discuss the HIF questions below.

Shape a specific object from modeling clay

Fold a piece of paper and cut out paper dolls

Lace and tie a shoe

Hindsight Questions
• How difficult was the activity to do (blindfolded/one handed)? Why?

Insight Questions
• How would you feel if you lost your (sight/hand) tomorrow?
• What would you do?
• How would you want people to treat you?

Foresight Questions
• What qualities do people who learn to live with disabilities have that you would like to have?

Discussion Opportunity: While different people may respond to similar experiences differently the basic experience is essentially the same. For example, the inability to see creates a difficulty for anyone who experiences the loss of sight. For people who lose their sight after having had it, the experience can be frightening. People who do not have full use of their bodies still have the same needs and responsibilities of other people, but their challenges are greater. An accident can change a persons life in a matter of moments. Recognition of these facts should encourage each of us to be respectful of individuals who have to live with disabilities. Character Traits: RO caring, fairness, citizenship

ACTIVITY 74

INDIVIDUAL DIFFERENCES - MUTUAL NEEDS

Either in a small group, or as a class, brainstorm ways in which people are different and list them on the board. Then discuss some needs that all people have in common and list them on the board. Next, have your students help you identify ways in which the proper use of these differences can better help everyone to meet their common needs. Below is a sample of some differences, likenesses, and contributions they might consider.

Some Differences	Some Common Needs	How Differences Help Meet Needs
Gender	To be born	Requires both male and female
Age	All people have the same basic needs for food, shelter, clothing, health care, safety, love, etc.	Adults take care young then, in turn need help when they become elderly
Size	Food, clothing, shelter, etc. some have special needs, for example infants	Big people can do some things small people can't and vise versa, adds variety and interest to life
Knowledge	Language and math skills, how to earn a living, etc	Enables people to do different jobs, everyone needs to be taught by others
Tastes	Same basic needs for nutrition, protection from elements, etc.	Provides variety, interest, beauty
Shapes and colors	Same needs for food, shelter, etc.	Provides variety, interest, beauty,

Discussion Opportunity: Human life would cease to exist without the differences listed above. Unfortunately, some people are afraid of differences in other people. It is inconceivable to imagine a world in which everyone was the same. The nature of life requires that there be two different sexes and that they get along with each other. We all age, change sizes, and require some degree of knowledge. Moreover, people come in different shapes and colors. That's the way it is. But, no matter where we are in this mix, we still require food, clothing, shelter, etc. Not only do we each have these requirements, we can all help each other in meeting these needs. The better we are at it, the happier and more successful we are individually and as a whole. Character Traits: RO citizenship

ACTIVITY 75

THE DRIED PEAS IN CINDERELLA'S LIFE

A Brothers Grimm Fairy Tale Retold

She was of the sort who, over the centuries, have brought discredit to the title of stepmother. Arrogant, vain, and peevish, her soul was as small and hard as a dried pea. Under her charge were three daughters, two of which were her own and like her in every way. The third, she inherited from her second husband who, without any consideration for her feelings, died shortly after their marriage. She, of course, had no objection to inheriting his large estate, it was his daughter that was the cause of her affliction. This child, being of a sweet, kind, and generous disposition, was cut from a different mold than her own children, and these were qualities she only dimly understood and little appreciated.

Nevertheless, Cinderella was hers to raise and so she did. Not, mind you, as she raised her own daughters, but more like a servant. Nay, if the word may be said, more like a slave. Unable to bear the good qualities of the child, all the more because they reflected unfavorably on the qualities of her own daughters, the stepmother had assigned her the most undesirable and unpleasant tasks in the household. She was made to sleep in a small attic room with only straw on the floor, while her stepsisters had bedrooms with the nicest furnishings imaginable. She was given only rags to wear, while they were dressed in the most beautiful of gowns. While she worked from dawn till dusk, they pleasantly wiled away their days, preening in front of mirrors and pampering themselves with lotions and creams.

Of an evening, when chores were done, the young girl would often sit in front of the fireplace and read by its light. Though she only had two books, and these she had read many times, this was her chief pleasure in life. In sitting so close to the fire, she often came away with soot and ashes on her

clothes leading her stepsisters to call her Cinderella.

Now, it so happened that in the kingdom in which they lived, the king had decreed it was time for his son to take a wife. To help the Prince in choosing whom he should marry, it was announced the king was hosting a ball to which all eligible young ladies in the kingdom were invited. In preparation for the ball, the stepmother obtained the finest of dresses for her own daughters, but told Cinderella that, since she had nothing suitable to wear, she could not go.

Although, she had always born her disappointments without complaining, that evening, after her stepmother and stepsisters left for the ball, Cinderella fell to weeping. Not just a little bit, mind you, but big crocodile tears. So sad was she that only those who have seen a crocodile cry can fully appreciate how unhappy she truly was.

She had not long been in this condition, when before her appeared the most enchanting creature she had ever beheld. It was a lady, rather smallish and plump in size, dressed in a beautiful white gown with gold trim, and possessed with the gentlest, sweetest smile Cinderella had ever seen.

"I'm your fairy-godmother," she announced, "Why are you so sad my child?"

Through her sobs, Cinderella told her fairy-godmother all about the ball and why she was unable to go. Proclaiming it would not do for Cinderella to be at home alone while everyone else was at the ball, her fairy-godmother quickly set to work. She waved her wand over a pumpkin in the garden and it magically became a gorgeous coach. In a similar manner, four field mice became beautiful white horses and a rat with long whiskers became a bearded coachman. One more touch of her wand and Cinderella was dressed in the most beautiful gown she had ever seen, with magnificent glass slippers to adorn her feet. In what seemed to be but a moment, Cinderella was off to the ball in her horse-driven coach. But, just before leaving, her fairy-godmother warned Cinderella that, at the stroke of twelve, her coach would again become a pumpkin, her horses would return to mice, and her coachman, would alas, be once more the rat he had always been.

When she arrived at the ball, Cinderella's beauty so captivated the prince he could see none other. Together, they gaily danced the evening away until Cinderella heard bells ringing and suddenly realized they were chiming the hour of twelve. Panicked, she turned and, without so much as a good-bye, ran from the castle as fast as she could run.

The prince was bitterly disappointed when the only sign that could be found of the beautiful maiden was a glass slipper she had apparently lost in her flight. But, with a boldness and determination characteristic of of his station, the prince dispatched his servants to search the kingdom for the maiden whose foot the slipper fit, announcing that she would be the wife of his choice. Day after day, discouraged and disappointed, the king's servants returned without success. But, not all days are alike, and one happy day they knocked at the door of Cinderella and her stepsisters.

At first, things did not go well, for Cinderella's stepsisters behaved most rudely upon discovering the slipper was too small for their feet. Attempting to make a hasty exit, the king's servants excused themselves and started to leave. But, just at that moment, Cinderella entered the room and politely asked if she might be allowed to try on the slipper. Her stepmother and stepsisters vigorously protested. This, by itself, was reason enough for the king's servants to let her try, besides which, they were agreeably touched by her beauty and gentle manner. To their delight, her foot and the slipper were a perfect match.

Within the fortnight, a royal wedding was announced with all the festivities attending such an event one would expect. Cinderella, in her newly elevated station, was quick to forgive her stepmother and stepsisters, though of a truth, vengefulness had never been part of her disposition. For their part, Cinderella's stepmother and stepsisters began to discover a better side to their natures and, though dried peas do not soften easily nor quickly, in time, through Cinderella's kindness, they became fairly decent creatures.

Hindsight Questions
- How did Cinderella's stepmother and stepsisters treat her?
- How did Cinderella treat her stepmother and stepsisters after she became a princess?

Insight Questions
- How would you feel if you were treated this way by someone?
- Why do you think they treated her this way?
- What was unfair about the way they treated her?

Foresight Questions
- How are unkindness and disrespect hurtful to the person who is unkind and disrespectful?

Discussion Opportunity: Iwannit Now convinced the stepmother and her daughters to care about things. Biggs Bigger made that very important to them. But Eency Weency Tiny Too also led them to think little and care little about Cinderella and her needs and feelings. Judge B. Fore stamped in their minds the idea that she was not as good as they, and Nameit Blameit gave them reasons to be unkind. Fortunately for them, Cinderella was of a more caring nature and did not seek revenge when she became a princess. Character Traits: PR right; RO caring, fairness

ACTIVITY 76

MAC & ZACH AND THE BIRD IN THE AIR

by George L. Rogers

In the same house and on the same street,
Where Mayberry and North Avenue happen to meet,
Live the twin boys named Mac and Zach.
Along with their parents and a poodle named Jack.

They went to the same schools and had the same teachers,
They were taught the same rules and sat on the same bleachers,
But Zach was so different from Mac his twin brother,
It was hard to imagine they were born to the same mother.

For example, when Mac purchased his new BB gun,
He thought moving targets would be the most fun,
So he shot at a rat,
And he shot at a cat,
He shot at a frog,
And he shot at a dog.

Then he shot at a bird that happened to fly by,
And knocked the poor thing right out of the sky.
Mac even shot BB's at Zach his twin brother,
When he was angry with him, for some reason or other.

Accidentally one day, Mac shot his bare toe,
And he jumped in the air shouting oh! ooh! oooh!
Holding his foot he yipped and he yowled,
And jumped up and down while he cried and he howled.

But even with this, Mac never gave it a thought,
Of the pain he was inflicting on the creatures he shot.
So Mac went on playing the hunter and hunted,
Shooting whenever at whatever he wanted.

But the brother of Mac was a much wiser young boy,
Who knew out of things hurtful can come little joy.
For doing things harmful is never innocent fun,
And happiness from them is not likely to come.

So when Mac shot the poor bird right out of the air,
Zack brought it home to nurse and to care.
And when Zach brought the bird in and showed it to Jack,
Jack wiggled his tail while the bird simply looked back.

Then Zach put the bird in a little shoe box,
Into which he had laid a pair of his socks.
Zach gave the bird some water and food,
And he watched and he smiled while it warbled and cooed.

And in a short time when it was well enough to fly,
The bird took its place with other birds in the sky.
Zach watched the bird as it took to the air,
And was quite pleased with himself as it flew here and there.

Now tell me quick in voices low,
From what you've heard and what you know,
Of these two boys from Hackensack,
How are they different, this Mac and Zach?
If you can tell me, then do it right now.
Please give me the whatfor, the whyfor, and how.

Hindsight Questions
* What did Mac do with his new BB gun?
* What did Zach do to the bird?

Insight Questions
* Why do you suppose Mac shot his BB gun at birds?
* How were Mac and Zach different?
* How did these differences influence their choices?

Foresight Questions
* What did you learn from this story?
* Why is it important to care about other's feelings?

Discussion Opportunity: Mac is not a caring person. He is so interested in having fun with his new BB gun, he did not even think about how birds might feel when he shot them. On the other hand, when he shot at Zach, he was trying to hurt him. The Stink'n Think'n Gang has Mac in their pocket. But Zach is a more caring person. He is kind and considerate. By nursing the bird so it could fly again, Zach experienced a kind of satisfaction Mac may never know. For the satisfaction of injuring can never equal the satisfaction of healing. Character Traits: PR right; RO caring

BIOGRAPHY

A CHANGE OF HEART IN KALIGHAT

Forty or fifty students from the university had assembled. A young man was speaking to them.

"Some Catholic nuns have taken over Kalighat, the old pilgrim's hostel next to the Temple of Kali," he said. "They are gathering in homeless Hindu's from the streets of Calcutta to convert them to Catholicism. These nuns openly despise Hinduism by preaching Christianity under the shadow of Kali. They do it to those who are most weak and vulnerable. They do it to those who are uneducated and unable to see what's happening. They must be stopped! Now! Today! Follow me!"

The crowd of students roared their approval and noisily followed their leader down the streets of Calcutta to Kalighat. Arriving at Kalighat, the young man said, "Wait here. I will go in and bring out Mother Teresa, their leader. Then, if they will not leave peaceably, we will throw them out."

The young man turned and opened the door to Kalighat. Once inside, he was startled to see two long rows of starved, wasted, human bodies, most consisting of little more than skin and bones. Some, obviously near death. Many had not the strength to even sit. All were too weak to care for themselves. A heavy unpleasant odor filled his nostrils as he looked around at the dozens of people, all sick and dying.

In among the patients were four women in white saris. They went up and down each line, patiently washing and changing each patient. Where necessary, they took time to treat open sores and wounds. "Those must be the Catholic sisters." he thought. He watched the sisters joking and laughing with those patients who could respond.

Cautiously, the young man approached one of the sisters in white who was tending a man who appeared to be very ill. He saw the man take hold of the sister's hand. By this time he was close enough to hear the man whisper, "I lived as an animal in the street, but now I die as an angel, loved and cared for." The man smiled faintly, and then slipped silently away.

Almost embarrassed, the young man asked the nurse, "Is there no preaching here?"

The sister smiled at him. "Not with words," she said. "Kalighat is the home for the dying. Our mission is to outcasts like this poor man, those who have been discarded or ignored by others, and to bring them as much comfort as possible. If we cannot save them, and most we don't, at least they can die with dignity knowing that someone cared."

The sister looked at the young man and asked if he would like to know how Kalighat came about. He said yes.

"About five years ago," the Sister began, "in 1948, Mother Teresa started on a mission of love and compassion to the poorest of the poor. All alone, without any money, and here in Calcutta, Mother Teresa began by starting a school for children. It was not an ordinary school. She had no building, no books, no chalkboard or slate. She started it under a plum tree in the Moti Jihl bustee. She approached several parents to ask if they would like their children to get an education. They said yes. Her first day she had five students. She wrote in the dirt with a stick. Soon there were more than forty students every day. They were good students and wanted to learn. Then other Sisters came to join her and help in her work. Government officials and others who saw what she was doing contributed land and money. Now there are fifteen schools for the slum children in Calcutta. Most are in buildings. There is even a school for children from families with leprosy.

"As she was going about setting up the schools, Mother Teresa could not ignore the many people she saw lying in the streets, helpless and dying, with no one seeming to care or offer assistance. One day, she came across a poor lady whose body had been half eaten by rats and ants. She got a taxi to take her and the lady to a local hospital. The hospital was reluctant to take the woman as a patient, but Mother Teresa was persistent, and eventually the hospital accepted her.

"This was but the beginning. Unfortunately, most often the hospitals refused to treat the patients Mother Teresa brought in. Of course, neither Mother Teresa nor the patients she brought had any money. But if the hospital would not accept these poor souls, what was Mother Teresa to do? She could not just toss the person back out on the street. So Mother Teresa rented a small apartment. Soon she and the other Sisters were caring for several patients in that tiny apartment. They desperately needed more space. That was when Mother Teresa approached Dr. Ahmed who made this building available to us. Here, we only take in the sick and dying who have nowhere else to go and who can no longer take care of themselves."

In the background the young man was suddenly aware of the growing sound of angry voices from outside. Hastily he excused himself and went to the door. As he walked out, he raised his hands to the crowd of students. Voices became quiet as they listened to what he had to say.

"Inside there are people who are sick and dying,." the young man said. "They smell from their own waste and rotting bodies. These are homeless people, no longer able to care for themselves. People who were dying in the gutters and streets who have been brought here to be washed, to have their sores treated, and to be fed. I will only bring out Mother Teresa and the other Catholic sisters on one condition. That condition is that you go home and get your mothers and your sisters to come down here and take over the care of these dying and decaying people. Who of you is willing to do that?"

The crowd was strangely quiet. Then slowly, one by one, the students began filing off, some going one way and some going another. Before long the young man was left alone. Then slowly, he too began to walk away. As he walked, he looked around him at the teeming masses of homeless people on the street, all dressed in tattered rags and begging for scraps of food. He stopped for a moment, looked back at Kalighat, then continued walking.

Hindsight Questions
- Why were the students unhappy with the Catholic nuns?
- What were the nuns actually doing?

Insight Questions
- How were the students being unfair with the nuns?
- Who really cared more about the well-being of the homeless, the students or the nuns?

Foresight Questions
- How can the Seven C skills help people understand each other better?

Discussion Opportunity: Judge B. Fore convinced the students they knew what was going on at Kalighat. Nameit Blameit pitted Hindus against Catholics in their minds and Biggs Bigger made them think it was a terrible problem. In this frame of mind they made very unfair judgments of the nuns and what they were doing. Moreover, it led them to care more about the idea of their religion than the people of their religion. The nuns, however, were not preaching religion, they were caring for people in need. In fact, they were working with such little resources that caring was about all they were able to give, but it meant a great deal to those who had come to believe that no one really cared about them at all. Character Traits: SR self-reliance; Ro caring, citizenship

---

ACTIVITY 78

DICK WHITTINGTON AND HIS CAT

An English Fairy Tale *Dick Whittington's Cat* Retold

Dick Whittington was an orphan boy from the country. He had arrived in London penniless and hungry. He knocked at a house to beg for food. The cook was telling Dick to go away when the man of the house returned home.

Mr. Fitzwarren was a kind man, and when he heard Dick's story he invited Dick in for something to eat and offered him a job as the cook's helper. The cook was not pleased and proceeded to make life miserable for Dick. Among other things, she moved him into an old dirty attic overrun with mice. The mice were so bad, Dick couldn't sleep at nights so saved his money and bought a cat. He named her Tabby. Tabby proved to be a good mouser, and even more, a good friend for Dick, who was often lonely.

One day, Mr. Fitzwarren gathered all his servants around him. He told them he was sending a merchant vessel, "the good ship *Unicorn*," to foreign lands to sell and trade goods. He invited his servants to each send something they owned to be sold or traded, with the offer that they could keep whatever they received in return for what they sent. "Tabby" was all that Dick owned, and with much sadness, he sent her to go with the ship's captain.

The ship was gone for many months, and for a long time it was believed the *Unicorn* had gone down in the ocean. Dick, thinking she had died, felt very badly about having sent Tabby with the ship.

The cook treated Dick so cruelly, and without Tabby he was so lonely, that one night he decided to run away. But Dick had not gone very far when he heard the bells of old Bows Church begin to ring. As the bells rang, he thought he heard them say: "Turn again, Whittington, Thrice Lord Mayor of London Town" repeated over and over. On hearing this, Dick decided that he could bear the cook's cruelty a while longer and

returned home before he was missed.

One day, a few weeks later, there was great excitement. The *Unicorn* had safely returned home and Mr. Fitzwarren invited his servants to hear the captain's strange tale.

"We had been upon the sea for many days when we were caught in a terrible storm." the Captain began. "For a while we did not think we would make it, then the storm let up. After drifting in the fog for a while, we sighted land. We did not know where we were, but when we made port and sent ashore, we discovered that we were in Barbary, among the Moors, a people we had never seen before.

We were treated kindly, and traded with them for better prices than we had found in any other place we had been. While there, the king and queen of Barbary invited us to dinner. The palace was beautiful, but as the dinner was set before us, before we could eat it, large rats and mice ran out from all directions and made off with the food. When we asked why the king put up with it, he told us he did not know how to get rid of them.

I remembered that Dick's cat, Tabby, was still on the ship and sent one of my men to get her. No sooner had he returned with Tabby than she set upon the mice and quickly began to get rid of them. At first the queen was afraid of Tabby, but when I placed Tabby in her lap and Tabby began to purr, she thought what a wonderful animal Tabby was. The king and queen agreed that such a wonderful animal must be worth a great deal so they loaded my ship with many fine goods in return."

When the captain completed his story, Mr. Fitzwarren asked Dick to step forward. "You are now a young man of great wealth," said Mr.

Fitzwarren, "and I hope with all my heart that you may enjoy it through a long life." When Dick finally got his voice, he pronounced generous gifts for everyone he knew, from the captain to the cook.

With his new wealth, Dick bought some new clothes and went to school. Years passed and Dick became a fine young man. He married Mr. Fitzwarren's daughter, Alice, who he had loved since he was a boy, and eventually became sheriff and was elected three times as Lord Mayor of London town. Though Dick became a man of wealth and high position, he never forgot the needs of the poor and was always generous in his efforts to help them, remembering always that his own good fortune was due to the kindness of Mr. Fitzwarren and to his faithful cat, Tabby.

Hindsight Questions
- How would you describe Dick Wittingham as a young boy?
- What kind of a person was Dick after he became wealthy and successful?

Insight Questions
- What is the moral of this story?
- What benefit did the cook get from treating Dick badly?
- What may the cook have lost by treating him badly?
- Which members of the Stink'n Think'n Gang were working on the cook?

Foresight Questions
- Why was it a good thing Dick did not run away?
- Why is it sometimes a good idea to stick out a bad situation?

ACTIVITY 79

WHICH IS BEST?

Present the following situations to your students, or substitute situations from your own experience. After each situation ask and discuss questions like the following:
- Which individuals in the story demonstrated respect/disrespect?
- Why do you think each character acted this way?
- How would you feel if someone did this to you?

1. Juanita saw Carlos on the ground. Three boys were throwing dirt clods at him. She angrily chased the boys away and and told them to leave Carlos alone.
2. Wanting to get a good seat, Emil pushed in at the head of the line. Seeing where Emil went, his friend Hue decided not to join him and went to the end of the line.
3. Tough McGrough pushed Bobby down. "Hey Bobby, baby, wann'a make some'n of it?" he said. Two boys who did not know Bobby but who saw what happened came over and said, "Leave him alone, Tough, that stuff doesn't go around here."
4. As the awkward little girl came across the finish line, Perry began chanting, "Myrtle's a turtle!" "Myrtle's a turtle!" Soon all the other kids joined in but Melissa. Melissa hurried over to Myrtle and said, "Great job, Myrtle! You made it! Don't mind them, they're not worth listening to."

Discussion Opportunity: One of the specialties of the Stink'n Think'n Gang is to get people to act rudely and be unkind to others. Criticism, Control, and Correction are three C skills you need to overcome their influence, whether you are tempted to be unkind to others or attempting to deal with someone who has been unkind to you. Character Traits: RO caring, fairness, citizenship

BIOGRAPHY

THE ORPHANAGE OF MADAME NGAI

The year was 1946. Ho Chi Minh was leading rebel forces in a rebellion against the French for control of Vietnam. In the village of Thanh Hoa, there had been heavy fighting and dead bodies lay everywhere. Children had been abandoned on the roadway to die alongside their parents.

Madam Ngai walked along the roadway gathering together small children who were still alive. Some were sitting helplessly beside their dead parents, others were wandering aimlessly about, confused and not knowing what to do.

Carrying those who could not walk, and leading the others, she took the children back to what was left of her house. Before the fighting, she had lived in a large and lovely house, but now not much of it was left. Nevertheless, it would have to do.

Madam Ngai's husband had been killed in the first month of fighting. But Madam Ngai and her servants took care of the children. When the fighting started around Thanh Hoa again, she knew that she must take the children and leave.

She gathered her jewelry and what money she had and moved the children to the village of Nam Dinh. By now she was caring for six hundred children. She bought a house and provisions to take care of the children. Unfortunately,

because of the fighting, within two years they had to move again, only by this time she had a thousand children. As the fighting shifted from one place to another, Madam Ngai had to move her thousand children five different times.

In Haiphong, the buildings and grounds were simple, only a small house with two rooms on the first floor and two on the second. There was no electricity or plumbing. Most of the children slept on hard beds in large open areas with roofs over them. A canvas was dropped over the sides to prevent the water from getting in during the monsoon rains.

Yet for all the lack of conveniences, the children were well scrubbed, well fed, and happy. Madam Ngai loved every child. Somehow, under her tender care, even in the most difficult circumstances, they prospered.

Of course, taking care of a thousand children is more than one person can do alone. One of Madam Ngai's talents was finding people with the means and the ability to help. One of those who proved to be most helpful was Tom Dooley, a famous medical doctor. He related the above story of Madam Ngai in his book *"Deliver Us From Evil."*

Hindsight Questions
- Why were these children orphaned?

Insight Questions
- What would have happened to these children if Madam Ngai had not cared about them?

Foresight Questions
- Why is it important for people to care about one another?

Discussion Opportunity: Madam Ngai was surrounded by people who cared about politics and power, but little about people. She cared about people, especially children. The Stink'n Think'n Gang had a great hold on the soldiers who fought in the battle. Under Eency Weency Tiny Too's influence, they hardly noticed the children who were left in the wreckage of their war. Character Traits: SR self-reliance; RO caring, citizenship

---

CHOOSING TO BE TRUSTWORTHY

Section Six

LEARNING OBJECTIVES FOR SECTION SIX

Recognize the need to be honest with ourselves

Recognize the need to be honest in relations with others

Appreciate two qualities that create trustworthiness

    Honesty

    Dependability

Desire to be trustworthy

SECTION OVERVIEW

"Trustworthy"—what a wonderful word! It means to be dependable and reliable, worthy of trust. It means to be safe, honest, and true, something to be counted on. In this section, the most important message we are communicating to youth are the many benefits of being trustworthy.

Trust is the basis of all human relations and is the foundation on which freedom rests. To the extent there is a lack of trust, there must be laws to protect us. To the extent there are laws to protect us, there is loss of freedom.

Of the great disappointments in life, none are more vexing than to have a loved one or friend violate our trust. At the same time, few things are more wearing than to have to constantly be on guard against one's associates. The great blessing of living among a law-abiding people is that we are able to live and move with some degree of safety and protection. As the proportion of people who are not law abiding increases, so also the risks and difficulties of daily living increase.

The key ingredient in trustworthiness is honesty. If we can see a thing for what it is, we can know better what to think about it and judge more accurately what to do about it. Where we get into trouble is when we trust those we ought not. Should we happen to become among those who can't be trusted by others, we become a danger to ourselves as well. To trust our own judgment and choices when others cannot is to trust that which ought not to be trusted.

Benjamin Franklin once wrote, "We can never choose evil, as evil, but under the appearance of an imaginary good." The very nature of dishonesty is that we must first practice it on ourselves before we can practice it on others. The process of altering or repressing truth so undermines human relations and so weakens the mortar of intelligent action as to render those affected by it exposed and vulnerable. Those who are unworthy of trust find themselves unable to trust others. There is no place nor any persons among whom they can be wholly safe. Required to live by their wits, they must be always on the defensive and are constantly subject to exposure and ruin.

While we may not always be able to know who else we may trust, it is essential to always be able to trust ourselves and to know that we will never willingly violate the trust of others.

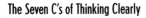

ACTIVITY 81

FOUR SHORT PUPPET PLAYS

ADVANCE PREPARATION: *Make simple paper plate or finger puppets, or use puppets you already have.*

81-1 —————————————— Mother and Patty —————————————

MOTHER: "Patty, where did you get that doll?"

PATTY (looking at audience): "If I tell her where I really got it, I'll get in trouble." Patty turns to her mother: "I found it."

MOTHER: "Where did you find it?"

PATTY: "Outside."

MOTHER: "Where outside?"

PATTY: "Under the bushes by the road."

MOTHER: "It's pretty muddy under the bushes, why isn't the doll dirty?"

PATTY: "I don't know."

MOTHER (sternly): "Patty, you're not telling me the truth. Now, I want to know where you really got the doll, and I want to know now."

PATTY (crying): "I took it from Susie's house."

Hindsight Questions
• What did Patty do to get what she wanted?

Insight Questions
• How did Patty hurt Susie? How did Patty hurt herself?

Foresight Questions
• How did doing one dishonest thing lead Patty to do another? (Stealing then lying)
• Why might it be more difficult for Patty's mother to trust her in the future?

81-2 —————————————— Mother and Noah —————————————

NOAH: "Mother, guess what I found."

MOTHER: "What did you find, Noah?"

NOAH: "I found a purse, and look, it has a lot of money in it. Can we tell who owns it?"

MOTHER: "Let's look inside and see if there is any identification. Why yes, it belongs to Mrs. Pindergast over on Vine Street."

NOAH: "Can we take it over to her? I bet she'll be glad to get it back."

MOTHER: "I'm sure she will. Mrs. Pindergast is quite elderly, and I am sure she probably needs this money very much."

NOAH: "Can we go now?"

MOTHER: "Yes, dear. Let me get my coat on."

Hindsight Questions
- What did Noah want to do when he found the purse?

Insight Questions
- What did Noah want?
- What makes you think Noah is someone you can trust?

Foresight Questions
- Why would Noah have reason to feel good about himself in returning the purse?

81-3   Penny and Peter

PENNY: "Peter, Joey's on the phone."
PETER: "Tell him I'm not here."
PENNY: "But you are here, Peter."
PETER: "I know that, but I don't want Joey to know I'm here."
PENNY: "Why don't you want him to know you're here?"
PETER: "I owe him some money and he wants it. Go tell him I'm not here."
PENNY: "I won't tell him that. You go tell him yourself."

Hindsight Questions
- What did Peter want Penny to do?

Insight Questions
- Why was Penny unwilling to tell Joey that Peter wasn't there?

Foresight Questions
- Why is it hard to trust people who lie to you?

81-4   Ruddie and Melissa

RUDDIE: "Melissa, you're cheating!"
MELISSA: "No, I'm not!"
RUDDIE: "Yes, you are. You're not closing your eyes all the way."
MELISSA: "Yes, I am."
RUDDIE: "No, you're not. I saw you look under your arm to see where everyone was going while you were counting. That's how you saw where Tommy hid. I don't want to play with you anymore. It's no fun to play with cheaters."

Hindsight Questions
- Why did Ruddie think it wasn't any fun to play with Melissa?

Insight Questions
- Why is cheating unfair to others?

Foresight Questions
- Why is it hard to trust people who cheat?

ACTIVITY 82

WHAT DID KADABE DO?

82-1 _____ **The Promise** _____

"I promise, mother," Kadabe said,
"At eight o'clock I'll go to bed."
But when the time of eight did come,
Kadabe still was having fun.

Then to his mother Kadabe said,
"At nine o'clock I'll go to bed,
I promise you that's what I'll do."
What does Kadabe's promise mean to you?

Hindsight Questions
*   What did Kadabe promise his mother?
*   What did Kadabe do?

Insight Questions
*   How good are Kadabe's promises?

Foresight Questions
*   How might Kadabe's broken promise be hurtful to him and to his mother?
*   Why is it hard to trust people who do not keep their promises?

82-2 _____ **The Chocolate Bar** _____

Kadabe wanted a chocolate bar,
Like those beside the colored jar.
"Who would know," Kadabe thought,
"If one I took instead of bought.

"Should I should or should I not?
Who will miss this bar?" he thought,
So first he thought and then he did,
He took the bar, then ran and hid.

Hindsight Questions
- What did Kadabe think?
- What did Kadabe do?

Insight Questions
- Why did Kadabe run and hide?
- What is wrong with taking things that belong to others?
- What lie did Kadabe have to tell himself before he took the candy?

Foresight Questions
- Why is it hard to trust people who take things that do not belong to them?

82-3   The Snowball

Kadabe made a ball of snow,
And gave the ball a hefty throw,
It hit poor Suzie in the head,
And when she cried, Kadabe fled.

When his teacher called him in,
Kadabe said to save his skin,
"I didn't throw that old snow ball,
It wasn't me, not me at all."

Hindsight Questions
- What did Kadabe do to Suzie?
- What did Kadabe tell his teacher?

Insight Questions
- Why did Kadabe lie to his teacher?
- How did one wrong thing lead to another?

Foresight Questions
- How does lying about what he did make the situation even worse?

82-4 _____ His Sister _____

Kadabe was told he had to share,
To eat it all would not be fair.
"Your sister wants some candy too,
Leave half for her, take half for you.

"Count the pieces," his mother said.
"And leave her share upon her bed."
He counted ten pieces there was no more,
So he took six and left her four.

Hindsight Questions
- Was Kadabe fair with his sister?
- What did Kadabe do?

Insight Questions
- What is wrong with what Kadabe did?
- How would you like Kadabe for a brother or a friend?

Foresight Questions
- How is Kadabe's choice hurtful to him and to his sister?
- Why might Kadabe not feel good about himself?

Discussion Opportunity: Kadabe is not a boy who you can trust. The Stink'n Think'n Gang has too great a hold on him. What he wants is so important, he will do anything to get it. He will lie, cheat, and steal to get his way. Eency Weency Tiny Too won't allow him to think about others and Biggs Bigger insists he think only about himself. Character Traits: PR right, accountability; T honesty, dependability

ACTIVITY 83

TRUSTWORTHINESS

83-1   Word Match

Prior to class, write the following words on the chalkboard: sick, rusty, clean, whole, bent, strong, wobbly, truth, broken, well, stable, weak, straight, shiny, dirty. *Ask your students, either individually or in small groups, to write each word on a piece of paper in 2 columns, with words of opposite meaning written next to each other.*

Hindsight Questions
*   Which of these words would you connect with being trustworthy? Why?
*   Which would you connect with not being trustworthy? Why?

Insight Questions
*   What is trust?
*   What does it mean to be trustworthy?

Foresight Questions
*   What happens when people can't trust each other?

83-2   Words I Would Like to Describe Me

Write the following words on the board; diseased, stable, broken, incomplete, secure, reliable, loose, honest, weak, defective, whole, strong, damaged, healthy, solid, safe, true, wobbly, trustworthy. Have your students select from this list those words they would like to have used in describing themselves and write these words in a column on the left side of a piece of paper, leaving two lines in between each word. Then have them write a brief sentence stating why they think this would be a desirable quality to have. When they have completed the activity, have them read their answers for each of the words.

Hindsight Questions
*   Which words do you want to describe you? Why?

Insight Questions
*   Why is being able to trust each other important?

Foresight Questions
*   What happens when people can't trust each other?

> **Discussion Opportunity:** Being trustworthy is a choice within each person's power to make. It is possible to choose to be trustworthy, no matter what anyone else does. In choosing the words we want do describe us, we are choosing the kind of person we want to be. The Stink'n Think'n Gang may try to convince us otherwise, but everything worthwhile is dependent on people being able to trust each other. Character Traits: SR self-understanding; T honesty, dependability

83-3 ——————————— Who Can Be Trusted? ———————————

Read the following paired situations to your class. After each, ask which person was most trustworthy and discuss why.

Truthfulness
Liedel said she did not spill the milk, even though she had
Gretchen said, "Mother, I'm sorry, but I spilled the milk."

Ted didn't want anyone to know he had stepped in the cement.
Al said, " I stepped in the cement, can it be fixed?"

Respect for Others
Tommy didn't like the little girl, so he pushed her down.
Eric helped the little girl up, and gave her some candy.

The girls ran to get away and hide themselves from Crissy.
Emily stayed and said, "Hi, Crissy! What's up?"

Personal Responsibility
Mindy had to be asked three times to pick up her toys.
Glenda immediately put her toys away when she was through.

Pam left the lid off the glue jar and the glue became hardened.
Louise was careful to replace the lid so the glue would not harden.

Self-Control
Elsie threw a tantrum when her mother said no.
Millie was disappointed, but didn't complain when her mother said no.

Elton took the toy car from Toby and hit him.
When Tad refused to share, Marty got another toy car to play with.

> **Discussion Opportunity:** Most of us know the difference between being honest and dishonest, respectful or disrespectful, responsible or irresponsible, or when people are out of control. But knowing and doing are two different things and that is the difference between being trustworthy and untrustworthy. When we do things we know are wrong, we have crossed the line. When we do things we have doubts about, we have crossed the line as well. Character Traits: T honesty, dependability

83-4   News Watch

Assign your students to watch news sources for the next several days to identify different acts of honesty and dishonesty. Have them make notes on the event and the consequences to those involved. Discuss the HIF questions below.

83-5   Story Time

Assign your students to read a book or watch a play, TV show, or movie and identify different acts of honesty and dishonesty. Have them make notes about the event and the consequences to those involved. Discuss what would happen if everyone dishonest, or what life would be like if everyone were honest and trustworthy. Discuss the HIF questions below.

83-6   Story Starters

Assign your students to write or tell the meaning of the following quotes. Discuss the HIF questions below.

Shakespeare:
> This above all: to thine own self be true,
> And it must follow as the night the day,
> Thou canst not then be false to any man.

Sir Walter Scott:
> Oh, what a tangled web we weave,
> When first we practice to deceive

Hindsight Questions
- What acts of honesty and dishonesty did you did you consider or observe in the activity?

Insight Questions
- Why do people sometimes choose to be dishonest?
- Why would someone choose to be honest?
- Why does it often require a deliberate choice to be honest?

Foresight Questions
- Why is it important to be honest and dependable?
- What happens when people are not?

ACTIVITY 84

OLIVER LEARNS A TRADE

Adapted from Charles Dickens' *Oliver Twist*

Oliver was running for his life. Behind him a crowd was chasing after him crying, "Thief! Thief!" Here is the story of how Oliver came to this unhappy situation.

Oliver was born in a workhouse, and for long moments his fragile little life teetered between life and death, but in this, his first battle with nature, Oliver came out the winner, though not by much. His mother was less fortunate and died shortly after holding him for a brief moment in her arms. Thus it was that Oliver was born an orphan.

With no family to care for him, Oliver was placed in a charity house. Mrs. Mann, the lady of the house to which Oliver was assigned knew what was good for children. She did not want their little stomachs to be overburdened from eating too much, so she spent only half their allotment for food. The rest she put in her pocket.

One day, when he was about the age of nine, Oliver ventured at mealtime to ask for seconds. He was labeled a troublemaker and apprenticed out to Mr. Sowerberry, the undertaker. In the Sowerberry home, Oliver was given a place to sleep under the counter where the coffins were made and fed on scraps of food that were of little interest even to the family dog.

Oliver tried to make the best of things, but soon found he was living with people who had it in mind that if they could make him unhappy, this would somehow make them more happy. One was Mrs. Sowerberry, a bitter, vixenish woman who immediately became Oliver's enemy for reasons she had not sense to understand herself. Then there was Noah Claypole, also a charity house apprentice, but not an orphan. In Noah's mind, being an orphan put Oliver one step below himself, and he intended to make the most of it. Finally, there was Charlotte who apparently felt it

would be nice to know that there was someone in the world who was more miserable than she was.

One day, all three began to torment Oliver at the same time, and he decided to flee his apprenticeship that very night. Oliver had no place to go, but London sounded as good as anywhere. It was along the way that he came into company with the Artful Dodger.

It was early morning. Oliver was siting on a doorstep in the little town of Barnet when he first saw Dodger. He had been walking for seven days. He was exhausted and weak from lack of food, and feeling very lonesome.

Dodger was about as dirty a young lad as Oliver had ever seen but had the airs and manners of a man. The Dodger wore a man's coat with the sleeves rolled up and a top hat on his head. Upon learning of Oliver's situation, Dodger bought Oliver some food and told him that if Oliver would like to accompany him to London, he would introduce Oliver to a gentleman who would give him a place to live and teach him a trade. This all sounded very good to Oliver.

Once in London, the Dodger led Oliver to a building that they entered by a secret back entrance. They walked up some rickety stairs to a room black from age and dirt. Inside was a villainous-looking old man standing by a stove, cooking sausages. In the room were four or five other boys and some beds made of bags scattered around the floor. The Dodger introduced Oliver to Fagin who welcomed him and introduced him to the other boys. After a meal of sausages, ginger beer, and hard bread, Fagin played a game with the boys in which he placed silk handkerchiefs, watches, and other objects in his pockets and the boys attempted to remove them without his knowing it. After awhile, Oliver was invited to play the game with them. For the next several days, Oliver stayed with Fagin while the other boys went out to "work." Each evening the boys showed Fagin the things they had made at work that day; handkerchiefs, wallets, watches, and even jewelry. Oliver thought these boys were clever to know how to make such wonderful things and he wanted to learn how to make them also.

Finally the day came when Fagin gave Oliver permission to go to work with the Dodger and another boy named Charley Bates. Oliver was excited, now he could learn a trade. The three boys sauntered along at a casual, lazy pace, going no place in particular. This confused Oliver who began to suspect the boys were going to deceive the old man by not going to work at all. He was pondering this idea when suddenly the Dodger came to a stop, put his finger on his lip to be quiet, and drew his companions around him.

"What's the matter?" demanded Oliver.

"Hush!" replied the Dodger. "Do you see that old cove at the book stall?"

"The old gentleman over the way?" said Oliver. "Yes I see him."

"He'll do," said the Dodger.

Quickly, Charley and the Dodger made their way to the old gentleman while Oliver followed behind in amazement, trying to understand what they were doing. The old man was absorbed in his book and did not notice the boys. Suddenly Oliver's eyelids opened wide in horror and alarm as he watched the Dodger sidle up next to the old man, reach into his pocket and pull out a silk handkerchief. Then Dodger and Charley began to run away at full speed.

In an instant the whole mystery of Fagin and the boys, of the watches, the wallets, and the handkerchiefs, unfolded to Oliver's mind. At this moment of realization, Oliver heard somebody call out, "Stop, thief!"

Frightened out of his wits, Oliver began to run. He continued to hear the words, "Stop, thief!" and soon realized that a crowd of people was running after him. When the Dodger and Charley Bates saw what was happening, they fell in with the crowd for a while and also ran along shouting, "Stop, thief!" Then quietly, the two boys slipped away from the crowd and ran in another direction.

Hindsight Questions

* What was the trade Fagin was teaching Oliver?
* What did the Dodger and Charley Bates do when the crowd started chasing Oliver?

Insight Questions

* Why would the Dodger and Charlie Bates join with the crowd in shouting, "Stop, thief"?

Foresight Questions

* What is the risk of associating with dishonest people?

Discussion Opportunity: The Dodger's instincts of self-preservation were so strong, he had no real loyalties to anyone other than himself. The Stink'n Think'n Gang had convinced him, Fagin, and the others that to get what they wanted, they had to steal it from others. This way of thinking made it difficult for them to care much about anyone else, even each other. Despite his own unhappy life, Oliver was able to rise above that way of thinking. Character Traits: RO caring, citizenship; T honesty

---

ACTIVITY 85

THE MOHATMA

85-1 _____ Gandhi's Vow _____

The boy with the little brown body was painfully conscious that he was smaller than other boys his age. His spindly legs and narrow chest did not allow him to do well in team sports such as cricket and soccer. He greatly admired boys who were good at such things and his own inadequacy made him even more shy and timid than he was by nature.

Young Gandhi was a Hindu and strictly observed the rules of his religion. Members of his caste were vegetarians who did not eat animal products of any kind, including eggs and milk. One day, Gandhi met some boys who had formed a secret society to eat meat. The boys felt that the reason Englishmen were bigger than Indians and

had the power to rule India was because they ate meat. The boys reasoned that if they ate meat, they too could become big and strong.

Gandhi joined the group and began secretly eating meat. Day after day, he looked at his bony legs to see if they were getting any bigger, but he could not see any difference. More important, Gandhi began to feel strong pangs of guilt and remorse. He was not only violating the rules of his religion, he was violating his own conscience. Gandhi decided to quit the society and do what he believed in his own heart to be right. He went to the Temple Vishnu and vowed that he would never again touch meat. To him, it was not only a religious duty, but a matter of personal honor.

Hindsight Questions
- Why did Gandhi feel guilty about eating meat?

Insight Questions
- How does going against one's own conscience weaken a person?
- How does keeping ones vows and promises strengthen a person?

Foresight Questions
- If Gandhi had ever broken his vow, how do you think it would have influenced his later life?

85-2 _____ You Should Have Told Me The Truth _____

The young lawyer stood before the judge. "Your Honor, I move that my client's case be dismissed in favor of the opposition."

"I commend you for your integrity, young man," the judge replied.

Gandhi then turned to his crestfallen client. "I'm sorry, but you should have told me the truth."

"You did right," the client replied. "I tried to mislead you for which I apologize."

Word quickly spread among the Indian community in Johannesburg that Gandhi was a lawyer who cared more for the truth than a high income. Gandhi explained his position to those who asked. "It is not important to win a case, but it is important to find the truth," he said.

Hindsight Questions
- What did Gandhi care most about?
- How did that influence what people thought of him?

Insight Questions
- Why to people sometimes lie?
- How did not knowing the truth weaken Gandhi's ability to to help the man?

Foresight Questions
- How does knowing the truth help a person make better choices?

85-3 _____ I Had Not Stopped Eating Sugar _____

As Mohandas Gandhi left the gathering, he was approached by an anxious young woman.

"Mohatma," she pleaded, "I need your help. My son is ill. He has been told by his doctors that he must not eat sugar, but he will not listen. You he reveres. He will do what you say."

Looking into her eyes, Gandhi responded, "I will do as you wish for the good of the boy. Please return here with him in three months."

Puzzled the young mother promised that she would return with her son in three months. When the three months had elapsed, the woman again came to Gandhi, this time with her son.

Compassionately, Gandhi brought the boy close to him and said, "My son, it is not good for you to eat sugar. You must follow your doctor's instructions."

The boy reverently bowed his head and said, "If you tell me to quit eating sugar, I will."

Gratefully, the mother thanked Gandhi, but still puzzled she asked. "But why could you not have told the boy this same thing three months earlier?"

"Madam," Gandhi gently responded, "three months ago, I had not stopped eating sugar."

Hindsight Questions
- When was Gandhi willing to talk to the boy about not eating sugar?

Insight Questions
- Why do you think the boy was willing to do what Gandhi asked him to do?
- How did Gandhi's quitting the use of sugar strengthen his influence with the young man?
- How will the boy's resolve to quit using sugar strengthen him?
- What was there about Gandhi that enabled people to place complete trust and confidence in him? (He never asked anyone to do something he didn't do or wasn't willing to do himself.)

Foresight Questions
- Why is trustworthiness such an important quality to have?

Discussion Opportunity: Because of his complete honesty, with himself and others, Gandhi gained the trust and respect of an entire nation. Because he never asked anyone to do anything he had not done himself, they were willing to follow his leadership and example. Gandhi truly cared about his people and they knew it. Gandhi employed all of the Seven C Skills in his behalf. He refused to let the Stink'n Think'n Gang fool him. Character Traits: SR self-denial; T honesty, dependability

---

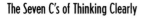

ACTIVITY 86

EVERYDAY DILEMMAS

86-1 _____ Julio _____

Julio's friends said, " If you want to be in our gang, Julio, you've got to prove yourself. Tonight we break into the gas station, and you better be with us."

1. Julio knew he shouldn't, but he wanted to be part of the gang, so after midnight he snuck out of the house and went to meet his friends.
2. Julio knew he shouldn't so he said, "No! I won't do that, even if it means I can't be part of the gang."

• Which choice did you think would be best for Julio to make? Why?
• Why might it take more strength for Julio to say no than yes?

> **Discussion Opportunity:** Iwannit Now will try to persuade Julio to be a part of the gang. Biggs Bigger will make it seem very important to him and Eency Weency Tiny Too will minimize the dangers and risks of breaking into the gas station. Criticism and Control can be of great help to Julio if he will let them. He needs to care about others more than himself, and to care about the future more than the present. Character Traits: T honesty, dependability; PR ownership, accountability; RO caring

86-2 _____ Lois _____

Lois promised her mother that she would come home right after school, but several of her friends were going over to Wanda's house and Lois wanted to go too.

1. After thinking about it for a couple of minutes, Lois decided to keep her promise to her mother. She said good-bye to her friends and hurried home.
2. Lois thought to herself, "I don't know why mom wants me home. I'll just go over to Wanda's for a while and then I'll go home."

• Which of these decisions do you feel is best? Why?
• What does keeping her promise require of Lois?

> **Discussion Opportunity:** Lois has made a promise. If she is a trustworthy person, her promise is a choice already made unless she can contact her mother and have her agree to the change. Character Traits: T honesty, dependability; RO caring

86-3 .... Travis ....

Travis looked at the pocketknife on the school playground. He was sure it was the one his cousin had lost when they were playing there on Saturday. His cousin lived in another part of the city and Travis knew he would not see him again for a while. Travis picked up the knife and looked it over. He really wanted a pocketknife like this for his own. Travis decided:

1. "I'll just keep this. If anyone asks me where I got it, I'll just say I found it and I don't know whose it is."
2. "I'll call my cousin tonight and ask him if this is his knife. If it isn't, I'll turn it into the lost and found tomorrow."

- Which of these choices is best for Travis to make? Why?
- How does bending the truth make it more difficult to trust someone?
- How would calling his cousin strengthen his relationship with his cousin?
- How would keeping the knife weaken Travis in other ways?

Discussion Opportunity: What does Travis care about most, the knife or his cousin? The knife or his character? Iwannit Now will try to get him to go for the knife. But by using the C skills, Travis will realize that the choice is more about what kind of person he wants to be than about the knife. The knife he will have only for a time. The kind of person he chooses to be will be with him throughout his life. Character Traits: T honesty, dependability; RO caring; PR right, duty, accountability

86-4 .... Marlene ....

Marlene was huddled with two of her friends, Ruth and Mona. Ruth and Mona were explaining to Marlene a plan they had for cheating on tomorrow's test. Marlene sat between them in class and they wanted her to help. They guaranteed her she would get an "A" on the test by working with them.

1. Marlene couldn't decide what to do. Her mind was like the pendulum on the clock they had at home, it just went back and forth. One minute she felt it was wrong for her to be a part of it, the next minute the idea of an "A" on the test sounded pretty good. Back and forth, Marlene went in her mind, unable to decide what she should do.
2. Marlene spoke up. "I don't want to be part of your plan. It's not the right thing to do."

- Which choice would be best for Marlene to make? Why?
- How is indecision like standing on a wobbly ladder?
- What principle could guide Marlene in making her choice?

Discussion Opportunity: There are many choices a person can make in advance. The choice to be an honest and trustworthy person is one of them. If Marlene made the choice to be an honest person, then she won't be wishy-washy when her honesty is tested. But if she doesn't make that choice, the Stink'n Think'n Gang has much more influence on her. If they can get Marlene to care more about getting a good grade than about being an honest person, they will have her where they want her. Character Traits: PR right, duty, accountability; T honesty, dependability

ACTIVITY 87

LENNY

He was a born athlete. "He had the body of a god and played like a god" one reporter wrote of him his last year of college ball. This is not to say that he didn't work hard, because he did. But his talent outshone all others on the court. Lenny was unquestionably one of the best players in basketball, destined to follow in the footsteps of Michael Jordan. He did it all. He possessed a shooter's touch and was deadly from the outside. Yet, he could drive for the basket and slam dunk with the best of them. He was a scorer and a star, but he was also a team player. He was idolized and admired by fans, and was well liked by both his teammates and fellow students.

Red Auerbach, the president of the Boston Celtics, had boasted that, if they got Lenny Bias in the draft and could keep Larry Bird healthy, the Celtics would be guaranteed the NBA championship. On June 17, 1986, in the second pick of the first round draft, the Celtics got their choice. Lenny became a Boston Celtic, the newest member of the number one team in basketball. From the very beginning, Lenny was treated as a superstar. He was now a national celebrity. Lenny was flown to Boston where he was met with luxury hotel accommodations, press conferences and lavish praise from Red Auerbach and sportswriters from around the nation. The next day Lenny was chauffeured by limousine to the headquarters of Reebok to sign an endorsement deal; one million dollars for five years. His agent claimed this deal assured Lenny lifelong security in one stroke of the pen. It was a level of security for which Lenny was to have no need.

By 10:30 the next morning, Lenny was dead. An overdose of cocaine. After returning home from his trip, Lenny went to his dorm. On the way there he picked up some beer and wine. It was time to celebrate. The celebration took place in a dorm room, next to his own, with two friends, the beer and wine, and an ounce of 88% pure cocaine. After three hours of snorting coke, Lenny went into a seizure from which he never recovered. This was not Lenny's first time sniffing cocaine, but it was his last. At the very moment when all the world had to offer was his, Lenny had accidentally taken his own life.

Hindsight Questions
- What did Lenny have going for him and how did he lose it all?

Insight Questions
- What is there about drugs that make them risky to use?
- What did a few minutes of pleasure cost Lenny?

Foresight Questions
- How could Criticism, Curiosity, and Control have helped Lenny?

Discussion Opportunity: Lenny was a gifted athlete who had a world of opportunity available to him. But Iwannit Now convinced him he wanted a little fun and Eency Weency Tiny Too led him to minimize the hazards of what he was doing. If he did not know, he could have known. Criticism and Curiosity could have told him that what he was doing was dangerous. Unfortunately, when people are infected by Iwannit Now they don't care about the risks. In this condition, people cannot even trust themselves. Character Traits: PR accountability; SR self-denial

INDEX SECTION

Index

Character Trait Cross Reference Guide

All the activities and stories in The Seven C's of thinking Clearly for Grade levels 2-6, provide opportunities to discuss various character traits. Some activities provide opportunities to discuss several character traits. The following cross-reference guide indicates the character traits each activity or story best illustrates. Character traits in the book are categorized as follows:

- **Personal Responsibility** encompasses the right to act, the duty to act, ownership of choices and actions, and accountability for actions.
- **Self-Respect** includes discussion of Self-Understanding, Self-Denial, Self-Reliance which includes Initiative, Industriousness, Persistence, Patience, and Resourcefulness.
- **Respect for Others** provides discussion opportunities for Caring, Fairness, and Citizenship which includes honoring rightful authority, and honoring the rights and property of others.
- **Trustworthiness** incorporates honesty and dependability.

❧

GREAT LESSONS FROM GREAT LIVES

Book One Grades 2-6

Book Two Grades 5-9

☙

GREAT LESSONS FROM GREAT STORIES

Book One Grades 2-6

Book Two Grades 5-9